The New
Enchantment of America
ARKANSAS

By Allan Carpenter

CHILDRENS PRESS, CHICAGO

ACKNOWLEDGMENTS

For assistance in the preparation of the revised edition, the author thanks:
CRAIG OGILVIE, Department of Parks and Tourism, State of Arkansas; BARBARA YARNELL, Department of Parks and Tourism, State of Arkansas; and MARCUS A. HOLLABAUGH, The Hollabaugh Collection.

American Airlines—Anne Vitaliano, Director of Public Relations; *Capitol Historical Society*, Washington, D. C.; *Newberry Library*, Chicago, Dr. Lawrence Towner, Director; *Northwestern University Library*, Evanston, Illinois; *United Airlines*—John P. Grember, Manager of Special Promotions; Joseph P. Hopkins, Manager, News Bureau.

UNITED STATES GOVERNMENT AGENCIES: *Department of Agriculture*—Robert Hailstock, Jr., Photography Division, Office of Communication; Donald C. Schuhart, Information Division, Soil Conservation Service. *Army*—Doran Topolosky, Public Affairs Office, Chief of Engineers, Corps of Engineers. *Department of Interior*—Louis Churchville, Director of Communications; EROS Space Program—Phillis Wiepking, Community Affairs; Charles Withington, Geologist; Mrs. Ruth Herbert, Information Specialist; Bureau of Reclamation; National Park Service—Fred Bell and the individual sites; Fish and Wildlife Service—Bob Hines, Public Affairs Office. *Library of Congress*—Dr. Alan Fern, Director of the Department of Research; Sara Wallace, Director of Publications; Dr. Walter W. Ristow, Chief, Geography and Map Division; Herbert Sandborn, Exhibits Officer. *National Archives*—Dr. James B. Rhoads, Archivist of the United States; Albert Meisel, Assistant Archivist for Educational Programs; David Eggenberger, Publications Director; Bill Leary, Still Picture Reference; James Moore, Audio-Visual Archives. *United States Postal Service*—Herb Harris, Stamps Division.

For assistance in the preparation of the first edition, the author thanks:
Consultant Curtis R. Swaim, Associate Commissioner of Education, Instructional Services, State of Arkansas; Vernice B. Hubbard, Supervisor of Reading; Winthrop Rockefeller, Governor; Arkansas Publicity and Parks Commission; and Arkansas Industrial Development Commission.

Illustrations on the preceding pages:
Cover photograph: Mountains near Hot Springs, USDI, National Parks Service, Hot Springs National Park
Page 1: Commemorative stamps of historic interest
Page 2-3: White River, Arkansas, Department of Parks & Tourism
Page 3: (Map) USDI Geological Survey
Pages 4-5: Little Rock Area, EROS Space Photo, USDI Geological Survey, EROS Data Center

Project Editor, Revised Edition:
  Joan Downing
Assistant Editor, Revised Edition:
  Mary Reidy

Library of Congress Cataloging in Publication Data
Carpenter, John Allan, 1917-
  Arkansas.

  (His The new enchantment of America)
  SUMMARY: Presents the history, resources, famous citizens, and points of interest in the state nicknamed Land of Opportunity.

  1. Arkansas—Juvenile literature.
  [1. Arkansas] I. Title. II. Series: Carpenter, John Allan, 1917- The new enchantment of America.
  F411.3.C3 1978 976.7 78-3786
  ISBN 0-516-04104-5

Contents

People still search for diamonds at Crater of Diamonds State Park.

A True Story to Set the Scene

HIS CROP WAS A GEM

The jeweler at Murfreesboro took the magnifying glass from his eye and looked up with amazement. Why, these stones looked like— but that couldn't be! The farmer said he had found them on his farm. Nothing like this had ever been discovered before in North America. He would have to ask the experts to look into this.

The objects in the jeweler's hand were not attractive, not very different from two rough pieces of glass. Yet they were to add a new episode to the many stories of enchantment of Arkansas.

About 1900 John M. Huddleston had bought a farm some 3 miles (about 4.8 kilometers) from Murfreesboro. One part of his farm disturbed him greatly; it was a total loss; crops simply would not grow on the odd blue-colored clay of this area.

From time to time he picked up unusual looking clear stones in the field. One day, according to Thomas Shiras, editor of the Pike County *Bulletin,* Huddleston noticed his baby playing with one of the larger stones, from which the blue clay had been cleaned. The more he looked at this stone the more extraordinary it appeared to him. He decided to ride to town and ask a jeweler to examine it. When he got off his mule to close the gate, and found another of the stones, he took that along also that day in 1906.

The jeweler was excited and puzzled. He told Huddleston that he thought the stones were diamonds, but he could not understand how this could be, since no diamonds of this size and quality had ever been found in North America. They agreed that the stones should be sent to an expert to appraise them.

The story is told that Huddleston had barely returned to the farm when the first of a long stream of people panted up—all wanting to buy his farm.

Huddleston was satisfied to take $38,000 for his land, and a group began preparations to mine the diamonds; they started their work in 1908, and Arkansas became the first and only state of the United States to have a diamond mine.

Looking over Arkansas from Mt. Nebo State Park.

Lay of the Land

AN EMERALD MOUNTAIN

"In 1721 some visionaries having assured the (Louisiana) company of an emerald rock on the Arcanzas River, Captain de La Harpe was sent to look for it . . . and he took me along as Mathematician," wrote Dumont de Montigny.

On the 9th of April, 1722, Captain Bernard de La Harpe wrote in his diary, ". . . we found some rocky country, and a league farther 'The Rock.' . . . we climbed this mountain and engraved on the heights, on a tree, the coat of arms of the King (of France). We saw on the west side several mountains and some beautiful countries.

"This (The Rock) is a steep mountain of clean rock made of limestone, which forms three mountains one after the other . . . to the right of the river; we named it the French Rock."

Dumont continued, "We ascended the river for more than two hundred and fifty leagues, without being able to discover this pretended treasure, probably because it existed only in imagination." It is likely that de La Harpe never expected to find a huge treasure of emeralds, but he wanted to keep the interest of his men.

Although the expedition failed to find wealth, it did add to the knowledge of the land that makes up present-day Arkansas.

It is especially interesting to know that there was also a smaller rock, on the south bank of the river. Both the larger rock and the smaller rock were widely known landmarks among the Indians.

The place is still the most notable landmark of Arkansas. For the beautiful country where de La Harpe's men received their disappointment now is the capital and largest city of the state. The smaller landmark gave the city its unique name—Little Rock.

The rocks not only provided a name for the city but, as the clever Indians pointed out to the explorers, the rocks marked the dividing line where the lowlands ended and the highlands began. The state today is about equally divided into low and high country along a diagonal line which U.S. Route 7 follows almost exactly in a long line across the state from the northeast to the southwest.

These two main divisions of Arkansas are known as the Gulf Coastal Plain and the Interior Highland Province.

The winding Arkansas River Valley sharply divides the Highlands into two mountainous areas. To the north are the Ozark plateaus, and on the south is the Ouachita (pronounced Washita) province. The highest point in Arkansas is Mount Magazine, rising to 2,823 feet (about 860.5 meters) in the Ouachitas.

The boundary with Louisiana to the south is a straight line; the boundary on the north is also straight until it reaches the St. Francis River, and then a bite appears to have been chewed out of what would otherwise be the northeast corner of the state. Another notch is gouged out of the southwest corner, also. This notch forms the Arkansas border with Texas.

The Arkansas-Oklahoma boundary is also a straight line that runs north from the Red River and then angles slightly to the west.

WATERS—FLOWING AND STANDING

Three rivers form portions of the various Arkansas boundaries. The mighty Red River bounds Texas and Arkansas and then cuts across a small part of the southwest corner of Arkansas.

Most people would say that the name of the eastern boundary river of Arkansas is obvious, but by a strange twist of political geography, Arkansas has two eastern boundary rivers. The St. Francis River separates Missouri and Arkansas. The obvious boundary and the mightiest of all river boundaries is the Mississippi, which separates Arkansas from Tennessee and Mississippi on the east.

A Mississippi River boundary is one of the most troublesome features of any state's geography. Over the years no one has known where or when the river would cut a new channel. Thomas Nuttall wrote in 1819, "The singular caprice of the river, as it accidentally seeks its way to the sea, meandering through its alluvial valley, is truly remarkable. The variation of its channel is almost incredible, and the action which it exercises over the destiny of the soil can scarcely be conceived. After pursuing a given course for many ages it has

12

Mouth of the Arkansas River *by Henry Lewis.*

. . . in many instances cut through an isthmus, and thus abandoned perhaps a course of 6 or 8 miles (about 10 or 13 kilometers), in which the water . . . at length becomes . . . a lagoon or lake."

Of this shifting river Mark Twain wrote in *Life on the Mississippi,* "Nearly the whole of the 1,300 miles (about 2,092 kilometers) of old Mississippi River which La Salle floated down in his canoes, two hundred years ago, is good solid dry ground now. The river lies to the right of it, in places, and to the left of it in other places."

In many places, surprisingly, the river no longer forms the boundary. Many loops of Arkansas land now lie entirely across the Mississippi River, while loops of the two states of Mississippi and Tennessee lie in what would appear to be Arkansas. This occurs where the boundary followed an old course of the river; when the river changed, the boundary was left as it was in these cases.

To keep the river within its banks, many devices have been used. Huge blankets of woven steel and concrete sections, called revetment mats, are placed along the shore to keep the banks from washing away. Similar mats were woven out of willow branches as early as 1850, but the force was so great they were not very effective.

High embankments called levees are almost the only protection during floods, which have been the terror of the region for ages.

In addition to the Mississippi, the main rivers of Arkansas are the White, Arkansas, Ouachita, St. Francis, and the Red.

The White begins in Arkansas, flows into Missouri and then returns to Arkansas. Henry Rowe Schoolcraft made an interesting comment about the White River in 1819—"Its waters, unlike most of the western rivers, are beautifully clear and transparent, being

13

wholly made up of springs which gush from the flinty hills that are found for more than half its length, within a few miles of, often immediately upon, its banks.''

Dr. John A. Wyeth said of the lowlands of the White River: "It is difficult to imagine anything more suggestive of helplessness and loneliness than one of these vast and seemingly endless stretches of cane with now and then an open slash full of tall and stately cypress.''

Near to the mouths of the White and Arkansas rivers, the two rivers flow so close together that the two channels have been joined by a cutoff; water sometimes will flow one way in the cutoff and then may change to flow the other way. In spite of this, both rivers continue their own way to empty separately into the Mississippi. Altogether Arkansas has 9,740 miles (about 15,675 kilometers) of rivers and streams.

The largest lakes in Arkansas are man-made; there are many large reservoirs in the state. These include Beaver, in the chain of lakes on the White River; Bull Shoals, also on the White, formed by one of the world's largest dams; Norfolk; Ouachita, one of a chain of lakes on the Ouachita River; Dardanelle; Millwood; Greers Ferry; Conway; Big Maumelle; Erling; and Hamilton, formed by Carpenter Dam.

Lake Chicot is the largest natural lake in Arkansas. It is of the type known as horseshoe since it lies in an abandoned horseshoe bend of the Mississippi River.

IN ANCIENT TIMES

At some time or other in the eons past, every part of Arkansas, except about 15 square miles (about 39 square kilometers), was covered by the waters of ancient seas. This is known by the fact that the surfaces are made up of mineral, animal, and vegetable matter that were deposited when the regions were under water.

The Ozarks and the Ouachitas were raised up, but experts say that they were formed in different ways at different times. Finally the last

14

waters left the regions that are now the highlands, as well as the present valley of the Arkansas River between them. However, the ancient seas continued to flood the lowland of present-day Arkansas. Gradually even these lower seas receded and the silt brought by the rivers began to create new land in this area that once was the ocean. These silt-deposited lands are known as the Mississippi Delta Country.

One of the well-known landmarks of Arkansas is Crowley's Ridge—a curving row of low hills cutting through the Delta Country from the northeast corner of the state to the Mississippi River near Helena. Geologists consider this formation to be very curious, and no one is quite sure just what caused this curving table of land to rise

Backpacking in the Ouachita Mountains

out of the flat silt. Part of it is sandy soil that seems to have been deposited by the wind and is known as loess.

Some authorities say that the Mississippi formed Crowley's Ridge by flowing at different times on either side of it in two different channels, which it also abandoned. Others feel that some force under the earth was responsible for lifting up the ridge, which they claim is still rising. During a period of 41 years in modern times, they say, Piggott Courthouse rose 1.34 feet (about 406 millimeters) in height. Whatever brought it into being, Crowley's Ridge is one of the unique natural features of the state.

Because the edge of the highland area once was the seashore, Arkansas has a variety of fossils from both land and ocean, but not much investigation of these has been done as yet. Many ancient animals were driven into the Arkansas region from the north by the glaciers, and their fossils have been found. Dr. Barnum Brown removed several thousand bones from the Conrad fissure, or cave, near Buffalo River. Several of these had been unknown to science before they were found. Fossils of Arkansas range from huge mastodons, plesiosaurs, and mosasaurs to small oyster shells. Petrified trees were sometimes used by early settlers for tombstones.

For many years people thought that the strange mounds found in pastures near Hamburg were burial mounds of ancient peoples. Now, however, they are thought to be geological formations. No one is certain just how these odd hillocks were formed.

CLIMATE

Arkansas generally has a climate that is without extremes of heat or cold. Rainfall averages about 45 inches (about 25.4 centimeters). Average snows range from about 10 inches (about 305 centimeters) in the northwest to 2.8 inches (about 7.1 centimeters) in the lowlands of the southeast. The growing season extends from 180 days on the high plateau of the northwest to 240 days in the southeast.

Opposite: The White River

Black Dog, chief of the Osage, painted by George Catlin.

Footsteps on the Land

WHAT THEY LEFT BEHIND THEM

He was a little man, almost a dwarf. When he died, his friends arranged his body with his knees against his chest. They filled a woven bag with a tool made of bone and a brush and they placed this at his back. They put a package of pawpaw bark at his feet and buried him in a dry cave, along with his faithful little dog.

He died more than 1500 years ago, but his almost perfectly preserved mummy and that of his dog, along with the objects buried with him, may still be seen at the University of Arkansas museum just as they were dug up at Brown's Bluff in Washington County.

The mummy was one of the dwarf-like Bluff Dwellers, once considered to be the earliest known inhabitants of Arkansas. They are thought to have occupied the region earlier than 500 A.D. Now it is known that a much earlier group were the Folsom people who lived in the region just after the Ice Age, around 10,000 years ago.

The Bluff Dwellers knew how to grow pumpkins, gourds, squash, and corn. They apparently did not know how to make pottery, but their baskets were woven so tightly they could hold water.

A more advanced people were the Marksville group, who lived on the plains. It is thought that in time they declined and later formed less advanced groups known as the Deasonville and Coles Creek peoples.

After a time, another advance came through the development of the Mid-Mississippian people in the northeastern part of present-day Arkansas. One of their accomplishments was the making of effigy pottery, shaped in the form of animals or people. A turtle teapot has been found, with the tail making the handle and the mouth the spout. These effigies are so similar to those found in Mexico and Central America that some authorities feel the Mid-Mississippian people must have come originally from those regions.

At about the same time the Mid-Mississippian people were making progress in their civilization, a group known as the Caddo people came into southwest Arkansas, possibly from the coast of Texas.

They enlarged and improved on the developments made by the Coles Creek people. Their leading families followed the practice of many early peoples of binding the skulls of infants to flatten them, apparently as a mark of the aristocracy.

Some of the leading discoveries of ancient peoples in Arkansas were made by Clarence B. Moore of the Philadelphia Academy of Natural Sciences between 1908 and 1911. From the burial sites and the multitude of mounds dotting the Arkansas countryside, Moore took many interesting items—painted and skillfully carved utensils, pottery decorated in bas-relief, pipes for smoking, arrowheads, and other weapons. One of the most amusing effigies was a water pitcher made like a human head with the ears as the handles.

The most obvious things left by the former inhabitants of Arkansas are those mounds, small hill-like projections found in many parts of the state. These are sometimes burial places; some are fortifications; and still others are the foundations for temples or other buildings. Some are thought to have been built simply as refuges from flood waters. Many times contemporary refugees from floods have found safety on the tops of these mounds—a practical modern-day example of the contribution made by the past to the present.

The group of mounds found on the Arkansas River, about 20 miles (about 32 kilometers) downstream from Little Rock, is known as the Knapp or Toltec group. This group has been called one of the most important in the United States. There are about fifteen mounds that are enclosed on three sides by what seems to have been fortress walls.

More than forty thousand items, found in many mounds, are now in the collection of Hampson Museum at Wilson. This collection has been called the most valuable of its type in existence.

PEOPLE OF THE GOOD HUNTING GROUNDS

There has been much discussion about whether the Indians found by the early European explorers were descendants of the mound builders. It is generally agreed now that some of the Indian groups were descended from ancient peoples; however, most were probably distinctive races that died out or moved away entirely.

Early explorers found the region of present-day Arkansas inhabited by three main Indian groups: Osage, Quapaw, and Caddo. The latter, of course, were the descendants of the prehistoric Caddo. They were a peace-loving agricultural people, although when they did go on the warpath they were described by Spanish explorers as the best fighting people. They are said to have reached a high peak of culture and artistic ability.

Even into the 1800s the Caddo were greatly respected by all their Indian neighbors, and they dominated at least a dozen groups of the region over whom they held great influence. They all spoke the Caddo language, and looked up to them, and joined them in all their wars. The Caddo had racial ties with many western groups, including the Wichita, Pawnee, and Arikara.

N. Joutel, a member of an exploring party in 1687, described a Caddo village of the time: ". . . We saw several Cottages at certain Distances, straggling up and down as the Ground happens to be fit for Tillage. The Field lies about the Cottage, and at other Distances there are other large Huts, not inhabited, but only serving for publick Assemblies, either upon Occasion of Rejoycing, or to consult about Peace and War.

"The cottages that are inhabited, are not each of them for a private Family, for in some of them are fifteen or twenty, each of which has its Nook or Corner, Bed and other Utensils to its self . . . they have Nothing in Common besides the Fire, which is in the Midst of the Hut, and never goes out . . . The Cottages are round at the Top, after the manner of the Bee-Hive."

After the Europeans came, the Caddo fell on hard times. A report to President Thomas Jefferson in 1805 says, "They have lived where they now do only five years. The first year they moved there the smallpox got amongst them and destroyed nearly one half of them . . . Two years ago they had the measles . . . The whole number of what they call warriors of the ancient Caddo nation, is now reduced to about an hundred, who are looked upon somewhat like Knights of Malta, or some distinguished military order."

The remaining Caddo tribesmen were moved from present-day Arkansas in 1835.

The Quapaw gave Arkansas its name. They are thought to be of Sioux background, coming originally from the Ohio region. They made their way down the Mississippi River, and so took the name Ugakhpah, which means downstream people. As this name was passed from one European visitor to another it began to change in two different ways. The word Ugakhpah finally became both Quapaw and Arkansas.

The French pronounced the name as if it were spelled Oo-gaq-pa, which the Algonquin Indians pronounced as Oo-ka-nas-sa; Marquette wrote it as Arkansoa; La Salle wrote Akansa; De Tonti, Arkancas; and La Harpe, Arkansas, the present spelling.

Thomas Nuttall gave an account of what must certainly be one of the world's most unusual battles. This took place between the Quapaw and the Chickasaw, who lived east of the Mississippi. "The Chicasaws, instead of standing their ground, were retreating before the Quapaws . . . in consequence of the want of ammunition. The latter understanding the occasion . . . desired the Chicasaws to land on an adjoining sand-beach of the Mississippi . . . . The chief of the Quapaws then ordered all his men to empty their powder-horns into a blanket, after which he divided the whole with a spoon, and gave the half to the Chicasaws. They then proceeded to the combat."

Eventually the Quapaw gave up their enormous area stretching between the Red and the Arkansas rivers.

After wandering homeless and in poverty, they asked for help. John Pope, then territorial governor, sent their request to Washington, saying, "They are a kind of inoffensive people and aid the Whites in picking out their cotton and furnishing them with game. I have heard but one sentiment expressed in this territory with regard to this tribe, that of kindness and a desire that they should be permitted to live among us; I would be particularly gratified to be authorized to assign them a township on this river (the Arkansas)."

Nothing came of the request, and the Quapaw finally moved to Oklahoma.

Few of the Osage made their homes permanently in Arkansas, but

they often swept into the region to hunt or fish. They made merciless raids on villages of other Indians, and later on the settlements after the Europeans came to the region. After their raids the Osage would hurry back to their homes in the hills.

A FEW STRAGGLERS

In 1541, after wandering over much of the southeastern United States and losing almost half of his 600 men, Spanish explorer Hernando de Soto managed to cross the Mississippi River and reached present-day Arkansas. There has been much argument as to just where he landed, but it is now generally agreed it was about 20 miles (about 32 kilometers) south of present-day Helena. He probably visited Pacaha, the Indian village on the site of Helena.

The vast expedition, with what was left of its 200 horses, herds of cattle, mules and hogs, bloodhounds to track the Indian slaves, and greyhounds to run them down, wandered through Arkansas for about a year. They visited the mouth of the St. Francis River, came later to the place where Little Rock now stands, bathed in the waters of Hot Springs and began the descent of the Ouachita River. They spent the winter at the Indian village of Utiangue on a bluff over the Ouachita River. It is not known whether this village was near present-day Camden or Calion. After the winter they went on down the Ouachita and out of Arkansas.

It is incredible to think that 132 years were to pass before other Europeans would again visit Arkansas. However, wherever de Soto and his men went they left a legacy of disease and hatred for Europeans that stayed with the Indians always. Many once prosperous Indians never recovered from the ravages of de Soto's passing.

In 1673 the gentle Father Jacques Marquette and fur-trader Louis Jolliet paddled their canoes down the Mississippi River and reached the mouth of the Arkansas River in the first long voyage of explora-

La Salle claims Arkansas, *a painting by George Catlin.*

tion on the river. They thought they were close to the mouth of the Mississippi, but the kindly Quapaw warned them that the mouth was still a long distance, through territory of unfriendly Indians, so the explorers turned back.

In 1682, Robert Cavalier, Sieur de La Salle, followed the route of Marquette and Jolliet, and reached the Arkansas' mouth on March 13. His assistant Henri de Tonti wrote, "In the fog from the right bank, we heard the Indian war cries and beat of drums. M. de la Salle did not doubt there was a village. We came upon it . . . and we were well treated and given a cabin for our stay. M. de la Salle took possession of the land in the name of his Christian majesty. It can be said that these savages (Quapaw) were the best of all we had ever seen . . . They had fish in abundance, roosters and chickens, and several kinds of unknown fruits."

La Salle did find the mouth of the Mississippi and named the region Louisiana in honor of the French monarch; then they returned up the Mississippi to present-day Illinois.

La Salle intended to return to the Mississippi in 1685 by way of the Gulf of Mexico, but his navigators missed the river's mouth, and they landed in Texas where they made a settlement. De Tonti had been left in Illinois with instructions to come back down the river to meet La Salle. Since La Salle had missed his way, of course de Tonti could not meet him and he started back with his men.

A POST ON THE ARKANSAS

The Quapaw village at the mouth of the Arkansas River was so attractive that a number of the men asked permission to stay in the region. They constructed a crude camp, which became known as the Post of Arkansas or Arkansas Post. This post, begun in 1686, proved to be the first permanent European settlement, not only in Arkansas but also in all the lower Mississippi Valley. De Tonti has become known as the Father of Arkansas.

The next summer one of the strangest encounters in American history took place. Six gaunt and weary Frenchmen, led by a man named Joutel, staggered into Arkansas Post. Joutel wrote, "We discovered a great cross, and at a small distance from it a house built after the French fashion. We knelt down . . . to give thanks to the Divine Goodness for having conducted us so happily."

La Salle had been killed by one of his men; his Texas settlement had failed, and these six survivors were fighting their way across the wilderness to try to get back to civilization. They might well have given thanks for accidentally stumbling onto the only outpost in half a continent.

For almost eighty years, Arkansas Post remained the only outpost in its whole vast region—a picturesque, brawling, romantic spot, a halfway point between the Illinois settlements and the settlements on the Gulf of Mexico.

John Law, a banker from Scotland who lived in France, obtained the rights to Louisiana and concocted a grandiose scheme to exploit the vast region for the benefit of his stockholders—a plan that came to be known as the Mississippi Bubble. Among other projects, Law planned to make the region around Arkansas Post his own private principality; he shipped 500 blacks to the post in 1719 and a year later 800 European settlers followed.

They did not know how to get along in the wilderness, and the entire group had to live almost entirely on the charity of the Indians. When Law's Mississippi Bubble burst, he fled from France, and as soon as the settlers heard of this they abandoned the post and went to New Orleans. By 1722 there were only 47 people left at Arkansas Post.

In 1763 France gave the entire Louisiana Territory to Spain, but about the only change at Arkansas Post was the change of name to Fort Charles III. An interesting description by Captain Philip Pittman, a Briton, in 1770 pictures Arkansas Post as ". . . situated three leagues up the river Arcansas . . . the sides of the interior polygon (of the fort's walls) are about 1800 feet (about 548 meters), and one 3-pounder (1.4 kilogram) is mounted in the flanks and faces of each bastion . . . The fort stands about 200 yards (about 183 meters) from the waterside and is garrisoned by a captain, a lieutenant, and 30 French soldiers, including sergeants and corporals.

There are eight houses within the fort, occupied by as many families . . . These people subsist mostly by hunting, and every season sent to New Orleans great quantities of bear's oil, tallow, salted buffalo meat, and a few skins."

The post defenders and their allies the Quapaw had many brushes with the Chickasaw and other enemies. After a Chickasaw attack on the post in 1783, Jacobo Dubreuil, the post's commandant, wrote that he had to purchase "one cask of brandy to revive the troops . . . three rolls of tobacco to please the troops and volunteers who went in pursuit of the enemy."

A SUCCESSION OF EVENTS—SOME EARTHSHAKING

In 1797 the community of Helena was begun by Sylvanus Phillips. Three years later France again was given ownership of the great Louisiana Territory. French officials had barely arrived in the territory when France sold all of Louisiana to the United States, and American troops came in 1804 to take over Arkansas Post.

Wild tales were told about the wealth of the region. The United States Committee on Commerce and Manufacturers reported testimony on the "masses of virgin silver and gold that glitter in the veins of the rocks which underlay the Arkansas."

In order to find out more about the new region, Dr. George Hunter and William Dunbar were sent on an expedition that went up the Ouachita River in 1804, and spent some time in the neighborhood of Hot Springs. Needless to say, they did not find the region lined with gold and silver.

This may have been one reason why European settlers were slow in coming. The census of 1810 showed only 1,062 of them in present-day Arkansas.

It was fortunate that the population was small in 1811, when a series of earthquakes began. An interesting eyewitness account reported on the first earth shock: "The agitation which convulsed the earth, and the waters of the mighty Mississippi, filled every living creature with horrors . . . Directly a loud roaring and hissing was heard like the escape of steam from a boiler, accompanied by the most violent agitation of the shores, and tremendous boiling up of the waters of the Mississippi in huge swells . . . Sand bars and points of the islands gave way, swallowed up in the tumultuous bosom of the river . . . The earth on the shores opened in wide fissures, and closing again, threw the water, sand and mud, in huge jets, higher than the tops of trees . . . the river rose in a few minutes five or six feet (1.5 or 1.8 meters) . . .''

Smaller quakes continued for many months, and the land in the St. Francis region was changed into an area of lakes and swampy lowlands.

President Thomas Jefferson was first to propose that the eastern Indians who had been driven from their ancestral homes might find new homes in almost-empty Arkansas, and in 1817 the Cherokee signed a treaty to give up their lands in the eastern highlands.

There were already a good many Cherokee in present-day Arkansas. In 1808 Chief Tahlonteskee had led 300 of his followers into the valley of the Arkansas River, lands that had been given up by the Osage. Others of this cultured and advanced group soon followed. Arkansas became a center of Cherokee civilization.

Chief John Jolly became head of the Cherokee on the death of his brother Tahlonteskee and made Cherokee headquarters, Galla Rock, a model village. When he left the East, he wrote a government official, ''You must not think that by removing we shall return to the savage life. You have learned us to be herdsmen & cultivators, and to spin and weave. Our women will raise the cotton & the Indigo & spin & weave cloth to cloath our children.''

In 1819 Thomas Nuttall described the banks of the Arkansas as ''lined with houses and farms of the Cherokees, and though their dress was a mixture of indigenous and European taste, yet in their houses, which are decently furnished, and in their farms, which were well fenced and stocked with cattle, we perceive a happy approach toward civilization . . . some of them are possessed of property to the amount of many thousands of dollars, have houses handsomely and conveniently furnished, and their tables spread with our dainties and luxuries.''

28

The home of Lieutenant C.F.M. Noland, who delivered the first constitution of Arkansas to Washington.

American settlers, however, looked longingly at Cherokee land, and by 1829 the Cherokee were once again driven from their homes, to present-day Oklahoma.

In the years between 1810 and 1819 the non-Indian population of Arkansas increased to about 14,000. Arkansas appeared ready to be separated from Missouri Territory, and Arkansas Territory was organized in 1819, with James I. Miller as first territorial governor. Little Rock was chosen as the capital in 1820 and the seat of government was moved there from Arkansas Post.

A SOVEREIGN STATE

Settlers continued to stream into the virgin land. They struggled overland by oxcart or wagon, fought their way upriver in keelboats or were lucky enough to enjoy the luxury of newly arrived steamboats. A handsome state house was begun in 1833, to cost the staggering sum of $125,000. By 1836 the population had climbed above 50,000. Although many in Congress were unhappy about admitting a new slave state, the statehood bill at length was passed, and Arkansas became the 25th state on June 15, 1836.

Although the new capitol was not completed, the newly elected state legislature met there and the first governor, Colonel James Conway, was inaugurated there. Colonel Conway proclaimed to the legislature: "Fellow citizens, the date of our existence as a free and independent state has begun."

29

Right: Western artist Frederick Remington depicts the great trek to the west. Below: The Battle of Pea Ridge.

Yesterday and Today

TWENTY-FIVE YEARS BETWEEN

In the twenty-five years between statehood and the beginning of the Civil War, progress was rapid in Arkansas. The population increased eight times over. Factories and mills turned out meal, flour, lumber, cloth, and many other necessities. Use of gas for lighting was begun, and some cities were connected by telegraph. Churches, schools, and colleges were organized.

As one of Texas' neighbors, Arkansas took more than a casual interest in the growing dispute about Texas. General Zachary Taylor was sent to take command of Fort Smith. He made many preparations on the Texas frontier for what he apparently expected would someday be a war with Mexico. When that war came, he was ready, and his successes in the war paved the way for his rise to the Presidency of the United States.

Arkansas' Archibald Yell was serving in Congress when the war came. He resigned his position to take command of an Arkansas cavalry regiment. Yell was killed in a gallant fight at Buena Vista in Mexico.

Western Arkansas became a jumping-off place for those who hurried to find the gold of California. Van Buren and Fort Smith were principal outfitting points for the California gold rush forty-niners.

During the decade of 1850-60, the great and growing concern was the dispute over slavery. Arkansas was classified as a slave state. The increasing number of great plantations in the low country depended on slaves for labor. However, the farms of the up-country were smaller and mostly operated by their owners who owned few slaves, so that there was considerable division in the state itself over slavery.

CONFLICT!

Other states had seceded and seized Federal property when Arkansas seized control of the Federal arsenal at Little Rock. In spite of this, the convention at Little Rock in March, 1861, voted no on the question of seceding from the United States.

However, after the fighting broke out in South Carolina, Governor Henry M. Rector refused President Lincoln's call for volunteers and seized Fort Smith. With only one dissenting vote, a new convention in May voted to secede. War had come; troops were prepared and sent to other states where fighting already was going on.

Actual fighting came to Arkansas in March of 1862, in a battle that was to influence the whole course of the war in the Mississippi Valley. On March 7 and 8, 10,500 Federal troops under General Samuel R. Curtis met about 16,000 troops of the Confederates under General Earl Van Dorn in what is called the Battle of Pea Ridge. Historians generally consider that the Southern troops won the victory, but they failed to destroy the Union army.

This battle and that of Prairie Grove, beginning on November 28, 1862, were the largest of the war to be fought on Arkansas soil. Both sides again claimed victory at the Battle of Prairie Grove. Confederate General Thomas Hindman wrote that the enemy "fled beyond the prairie, leaving his dead and wounded . . . " Union General Francis J. Herron reported a few days later, "The victory is more complete and decisive than I imagined."

Federal forces occupied Helena in 1862, and Arkansas Post was captured on January 11, 1863, in the Federal drive to control the Mississippi. Using Helena as a base, Union forces started a drive toward Little Rock, and the capital fell in September. The state government had already moved to Washington, Arkansas. As Little Rock was taken over, one witness reported, "The Federal troops were well received in Little Rock after the first contacts were made, and the occupation throughout was marked by orderliness and courtesy on both sides. Many of the Federal soldiers remained in Arkansas after the war."

Pine Bluff was the scene of a battle on October 25, 1863, as Confederate General John S. Marmaduke began a drive to take the city from Federal control. Federal forces prepared for a siege behind a fortification made of cotton bales. Marmaduke felt he would lose too many men in assaulting this fortification, so he withdrew.

In 1864, the counties of Arkansas under Federal control sent delegates to a convention that set up a new state government at Little Rock, so for a time Arkansas had two civil governments.

The last major fighting of the war in Arkansas occurred when Federal troops moved southward to encircle Confederate armies in southern Arkansas and northern Louisiana. They captured Camden, but were soon forced to retreat to Little Rock. During this drive the Arkansas Confederate government had been moved to Rondo for a short time.

Fighting in Arkansas was officially ended May 26, 1865, with the surrender of General Kirby Smith.

AWFUL CONSEQUENCES

Sixty thousand men from Arkansas had served in the Confederate forces. They began to straggle back from the many battlefields where they had fought with bravery. They found their farms in ruins, without even mules or plows to put in a new crop, and their credit gone.

When a local storekeeper refused to furnish supplies on credit, one Confederate veteran wrote him this note: "Go to hell, Mr. Merchant, with your supplies. The woods is full of 'simmons, the vines is full of grapes, the 'possum is fat and slick, the coon is as good as ever; and we can live on these till springtime comes; then we

"Mustered Out" Black Volunteers at Little Rock, *May 19, 1866, a painting by Robert Guillemin, based on a sketch by Alfred R. Waud from* Harper's Weekly.

can live on blackberries till roasting ears come; then on them till the corn gets hard, and the old woman and boys can grind it on our old steel mill the Yankees left in the yard, while I hunt and fish.''

The former state government that had moved to Washington ceased to exist, and the government that had been set up under Federal troops at Little Rock became the government of the state. However, Congress refused to recognize this government in 1866, and it was declared illegal in 1867. Arkansas was put under military rule until the state would accept a new constitution and ratify the Fourteenth Amendment to the United States Constitution, which gave the vote to black people.

The new constitution and the government set up under it gave Republicans and those from the North, known as Carpetbaggers, control of the state under Governor Powell Clayton. Many of those in control were dishonest or unsympathetic to the needs of the state. Great hardship and much strife in the state came during the period known as Reconstruction, as the local people struggled to protect their interests. Riots broke out in many places between whites and blacks. Assassinations occurred on both sides. One of the last of these was the murder of Republican John M. Clayton, who had been defeated in a bid for a seat in Congress.

By 1872 the Republican Party was badly split. A liberal wing of the Republicans nominated the Reverend Joseph Brooks for governor; he also had the support of the Democrats; the regular Republican organization nominated Elisha Baxter.

Election returns of 1874 favored Baxter, but the Brooks supporters claimed there had been election frauds. A Supreme Court Justice supported this claim; Brooks drove Baxter from the statehouse by force and took over the governor's office.

Because both sides in this dispute actually took up arms, the affair has become known as the Brooks-Baxter War. Three Baxter supporters were killed in a fight near the Natural Steps when Baxter men tried to run a steamer, the *Hallie,* up the Arkansas with supplies for their leader and his forces. After the encounter the Brooks men took over the steamer that landed triumphantly at the statehouse dock. In another battle seven Brooks men were killed near Pine Bluff.

The matter was finally settled when the Federal government under President U.S. Grant proclaimed Baxter to be the legal governor. He called a session of the General Assembly. This created a convention to draft a new constitution, which was approved in 1874 and is still the basic law of Arkansas.

A MODERN STATE

In spite of the difficulties after the war, progress gradually accelerated, especially along Arkansas' western frontier.

Because the border with Texas was not finally settled until 1874, the region on both sides of the present border was a kind of no-man's land where outlaws and shady characters found they could escape from the justice of society. To the north, the border with the Indian lands in Oklahoma was also a region in which the forces of law were scarce or non-existent.

Here was all the flavor of the Old West. Gun fights sent many a spectator scurrying for cover on the streets of Texarkana, where the bars were full of the characters now associated with cowboy Western television. Hackett was another of the rip-roaring border towns, in which a dozen saloons often spilled their noisy brawlers into the street for fights with fists or guns.

Most typically Western of all, however, was Fort Smith. As early as the gold rush of 1849, the town had to pass laws to license, regulate, tax, or suppress pawnbrokers, money changers, public masquerade balls, sparring exhibitions, dance houses, fortune tellers, pistol galleries, corn doctors, muscle developers, billiard tables, and other instruments used for gaming.

When Indian territory came into being in Oklahoma, Fort Smith was headquarters for Federal justice in the territory, but the Oklahoma region was so vast that lawlessness was almost impossible to control.

Then into this situation at Fort Smith in 1875 came Federal Judge Isaac C. Parker. For 21 years Judge Parker dispensed the sternest kind of justice on the frontier. During the first 14 of those years it was not even possible to appeal his sentences to a higher court. Only the granting of clemency by the President of the United States could save a man condemned by Judge Parker, and he sentenced 151 law-breakers to hang, winning the nickname of the Hanging Judge.

Two hundred hard-fisted, hard-riding, gun-slinging deputy United States Marshals patrolled the judge's territory and called themselves the men who rode for Parker. So efficient were they that 83 of the condemned men were actually captured and brought to the gallows. However, the deputies faced such danger that 65 of them were killed in the course of their duties during Judge Parker's term.

When Judge Parker died in 1896, those prisoners remaining in his jail celebrated because they would no longer have to face the Hanging Judge. However, by this time relative peace and lawfulness had reached the frontier. Judge Parker had brought order to the West.

Right: A portrait of the hanging judge, Isaac Parker. Below: The gallows that Judge Parker used to bring order to the frontier area.

A short-lived gold boom at Golden City in 1886 caused a flurry of excitement. One so-called expert claimed the town was bound to be the Leadville of Arkansas. However, other experts said the gold fields had been salted (planted with gold from Colorado), and one expert said the ores contained nothing but pyrite.

Another kind of mining excitement struck Coal Hill in 1886. Private coal mining companies could lease convicts from the state prison to work in their mines. They received harsh treatment, working long hours for no pay and little food. Those working at Coal Hill staged an early version of a sit-down strike and holed up in the mine for 18 days. For food they killed the mules that hauled the coal cars; they barricaded the entrances and made cannon from iron pipe, with blasting powder and metal scrap for ammunition. At length they won their fight; conditions of convict leasing were improved, and the practice was finally done away with.

One of the state's extremely important natural resources was discovered in 1887. This was the mineral bauxite, from which aluminum is made. The community that sprang up around the discovery is now known as Bauxite.

A few years later another fascinating mineral discovery was made in Arkansas, although its commercial value was infinitely less than that of bauxite—John M. Huddleston and his diamonds. This has proved to be the only area in North America in which diamonds have ever been found in any quantity.

In 1913 a great fire destroyed 50 blocks of buildings in Hot Springs. Another disaster was the flood of 1916. The White River at Calico Rock rose and had a depth 51 feet (about 16 meters) greater than normal.

However, a far greater disaster was World War I; 63,632 Arkansas men went into service. Of these, 366 were killed. Camp Pike near Little Rock became so large that its 100,000 population was larger than the capital itself. Equally as large was Camp Joe T. Robinson near Levy. Another important military center was a pilot training field near Lonoke.

An Arkansas hero of the war was Private Herman Davis of Manila, Arkansas. He performed the impossible accomplishment of single-handedly killing four German machine gunners. This is considered to have kept an entire American company from being wiped out. At another time he picked off 47 of the enemy's gunners, catching them as quickly and accurately as he once caught squirrels on hunting trips near his home.

General John J. Pershing, America's war leader overseas, described Davis as the greatest hero to come from Arkansas and one of the four most distinguished heroes of the entire American force. He received high American and French decorations for his bravery.

In 1919 there were harsh racial encounters in the region around Elaine; at least a hundred blacks and an unknown number of whites were killed. The troubles continued for about a week, and rumors of large-scale insurrections were common. Finally the governor called out the National Guard, and order was restored. Large numbers of blacks were sentenced, but all of them were freed by the United States Supreme Court.

On a happier note, the first flow from the discovery oil well near Stephens came in 1919. This was the first time the state's great petroleum fields had ever been revealed. In 1921 there was another oil strike and a great oil boom at El Dorado. Oil was pulled from the ground as fast as holes could be drilled. The seemingly endless flow made many local landowners wealthy quickly.

The story is told of one newly rich family that decided to buy a mansion, although its owners had not intended to sell. However, the owner finally decided to take the enormous profit offered him for the house. As he was moving out he started to take down the family portraits from the walls. The wealthy oil woman objected, "Oh no you don't. Pitchers is furniture."

Sadly, because of the waste of the precious fuel, the El Dorado boom soon turned into a bust.

Another wild boom followed the discovery of oil in the Smackover area in 1922. Because greater care was used, the petroleum of that region was not wasted.

In 1922-23 there was a bitter strike of the Missouri and North Arkansas Railroad. Farmers who had contributed the land for the road and people of the towns feared that the road would be abandoned. Rails were torn up, bridges burned; one striker was pulled from his home by a mob and was hanged from a bridge of the railroad, before quiet was restored.

The town of Strong was wrecked by a severe tornado in 1927, and over 30 deaths resulted. The awful floods of 1927 were called by Herbert Hoover the greatest peace-time disaster in our history.

In 1930 Arkansas battled the great depression along with other parts of the nation. Then in World War II, more than 200,000 men and women from Arkansas were in service.

In the 1950s Arkansas made a determined and successful effort to attract new industry to the state. As part of that program, the state's official slogan—Land of Opportunity—was adopted in 1953.

During this period there was a growing crisis in race relations. In 1954, the United States Supreme Court had ordered desegregation of all schools as quickly as possible. Following this order, the school board of Little Rock planned to admit a small number of blacks to Central High School in the fall of 1957.

Governor Orval Faubus claimed that this would threaten the peace, and he placed National Guard units around the school, barring the blacks' attempts to enroll. When court orders made the National Guard withdraw, rioting mobs appeared and kept the blacks from the school.

At this point President Dwight Eisenhower made a move that has been declared to be a landmark in the relations of the Federal government with the states. He brought Federal troops to Little Rock and placed the National Guard under Federal service, which took it from the governor's control. Under Federal protection, the blacks were enrolled.

The President's action is generally considered to have established the principle that the national government could not tolerate defiance of court orders by local officials.

The publicity surrounding these events had made Governor Faubus a national figure, and he became one of the leaders in promoting the rights of the states. In 1964 he received an unprecedented election to a sixth term as governor of Arkansas.

However, in 1966 Governor Faubus declined to run. Popular

Winthrop Rockefeller ran on the Republican ticket. His election brought nationwide attention to Arkansas, and he took office in January, 1967. Much publicity was given to the fact that two Rockefeller brothers (Winthrop of Arkansas and Nelson of New York) were at the same time governors of their respective states.

Winthrop Rockefeller lost the election of 1970, and the state returned to the Democratic party. During the 1970s Little Rock became an inland seaport, the only foreign trade zone in the country on an inland river.

THE PEOPLE OF ARKANSAS

The simple days of the past are gone. There are few if any backwoodsmen left in Arkansas. Television antennas rise from the most remote cabins; universal schooling, radios, and newspapers are fast making an entire population almost as familiar with names such as India and Panama as they are with the nearest city. However, the memory and the flavor of the past still linger.

The famous story of the Arkansas Traveler has long given a misleading impression of the average Arkansas man. This story is one of the best-known pieces of American folklore. The story has been retold by Fred W. Allsopp in *Folklore of Romantic Arkansas.* A small part of the conversation of a traveler and an Arkansas squatter reads: "Traveler—'Sir! will you tell me where this road goes to?' Squatter—'It's never been any whar since I've lived here, it's always thar when I git up in the morning.' Traveler—'As I'm not likely to get to any other house tonight, can't you let me sleep in yours, and I'll tie my horse to a tree, and do without anything to eat or drink.'

"Squatter—'My house leaks. Thar's only one dry spot in it, and me and Sal sleeps on it. And that thar tree is the ole woman's persimmon; you can't tie to it, 'case she don't want 'em shuk off. She 'lows to make beer out'n um.' Traveler—'Why don't you finish covering your house, and stop the leaks?' Squatter—'It's been raining all day.' Traveler—'Well, why don't you do it in dry weather?' Squatter—'It don't leak then.' " The story goes on in the same vein.

40

Dancing to Arkansaw Traveller, *an oil painting by Casimer Gregory Stapko, based on the drawing* Arkansaw Traveller *by A.B. Frost, Hollabaugh Collection, Copyright 1976 by* Arkansas Heritage.

At one time many people had to depend on peddlers for the few things they could not make themselves. Later there were the "rolling stores" of rural Arkansas—trucks loaded with manufactured goods, groceries, and tools for farmers. They would take farm produce in trade and would return to their headquarters loaded with crates of cackling chickens and cartons of eggs.

41

In earlier times in the more remote areas, money was almost never used. Author William Monks writes, "When my father first located, beeswax, peltry, and fur skins almost constituted the currency of the country . . . A man thought nothing of buying a horse or a yoke of oxen, or to make any other common debt on the promise of discharging the same in beeswax and peltry, in one month's time."

Bee trees were an unusual source of wealth and were eagerly sought. When the bees were smoked out, the honey was put in deer skins with the legs tied in knots to keep the honey in. "The labor of the women then commenced. They would proceed to separate the honey from the beeswax, pouring the honey into hogsheads, kegs or barrels prepared for it, and running the beeswax into cakes, ready for the market, while the men were stretching and drying the deerskins."

Sir Henry Morton Stanley, the man who searched for Dr. Livingstone, wrote of the Arkansas planters that they were "stiff and constrained . . . They lived like princelings, were owners of hundreds of slaves over whom they were absolute except as to life or limb, and all other environments catered to their egotism. Though genially sociable to each other, to landless people like myself they conducted themselves as though they were under no obligations . . . Every new immigrant soon became infected with the proud and sensitive spirit prevailing in Arkansas . . . In Arkansas, to refute a statement was tantamount to giving the lie direct, and was likely to be followed by an instant appeal to the revolver or bowie."

Fortunately, dueling as a means of settling disputes has long since died out, but countless people in the past were killed or wounded in duels.

Today the people of Arkansas are almost all native-born Americans. While the progress made by the blacks of Arkansas must have seemed slow to many, others believe that the advances made during the last decades have been really extraordinary.

Most of the people of the state now seem agreed that the goal must be the best possible life for everyone in the new and rapidly advancing Arkansas.

Natural Treasures

THINGS THAT GROW

Early travelers in present-day Arkansas found an almost limitless expanse of trees, covering 32,000,000 acres (about 13,000,000 hectares) with the finest kind of virgin timber. In spite of all the use and waste that has taken place since that time, half of the state, totaling 20,052,926 acres (about 8,100,000 hectares), is still forest covered.

An idea of the wide variety of trees can be gained from the fact that there are in the state 60 kinds of hawthorne and 47 different kinds of oak, including the unique maple-leaved oak. The forests are divided into three main classifications—loblolly, short-leaf pine of the West Gulf Coastal Plain and Ouachita Mountains—the mixed short-leaf hardwoods of the Ozark Mountains—and the bottomland hardwoods of the alluvial plains of eastern Arkansas. Three national forests, Ozark, Ouachita, and St. Francis, have a total area of 4,059,555 acres (about 1,600,000 hectares).

More than 60 kinds of useful trees grow in the state. Some of the more unusual trees include the paw paw with its fruit-like bananas; the cork tree, one of America's scarcest plants, its leaves leather-like; and bois d'arc, also known as the Osage orange. The latter is prized above all others for making bows for archery.

Flowering trees and shrubs cover the countryside in spring with a spectacular display—tulip trees on Crowley's Ridge, splashy dogwood, dainty redbud, crab, wild plum, huckleberry, locust, silver bell, and wax myrtle all provide a blossoming preview of spring. The sweet scent of the azaleas (mountain honeysuckle) adds to the profusion.

More than 2,600 varieties of plants are found in Arkansas, which because of its location has many of the plants of the east, the deep south, and the western plains. The great variety is illustrated by the fact that there are more than 26 kinds of orchids, alone, in the state. An area near Helena is especially known for the near-tropical profusion of its plants.

ON WINGS, LEGS, AND FINS

Arkansas was once known as the Bear State, but only a comparative few of the lumbering animals now remain. To some, Arkansas might be known as the razor-back hog state, although no one has been able to determine exactly what a razor-back hog is. Old timers were apt to declare that they were so thin and their spines were so

The Fighting Arkansas Razorback, *painted by Robert Guillemin, based on the sketch entitled,* Hunting Wild Hogs in Arkansas *made in 1887 by Gilbert Gaul for* Harper's Weekly.

sharp, they could be used to shave with. If such a breed ever existed, it can no longer be found.

All 75 Arkansas counties have deer. Often the state leads all others in the number of trophy deer bagged. There is a special season for archers, and Arkansas permits crossbow hunting for deer. Other favorite quarry of hunters today are rabbit, coon, and squirrel among the creatures of the ground. There is a great deal more variety of birds. Possibly more of the stately wild turkey can be found in Arkansas than in any other state, along with large numbers of doves and quail.

Arkansas claims to be right in the middle of the duck road south. Some photographs show both ground and water almost solidly covered with ducks, which include mallards, pintails, and gadwalls. Stuttgart calls itself the duck hunting capital of the world.

Altogether, 312 species of birds are known in Arkansas, from the mountain birds to the wading birds of the lowlands. Few people will ever forget the sight of a white crane killing the fish he has just caught by banging its head against a cypress knee.

One of the world's more unusual fish is the strange alligator gar, said by some to be a living fossil. The most common game fish throughout the state is bass, and trout have recently begun to flourish in many Arkansas waters, where there also is a wide variety of pan fish.

The weird roar of the bull alligator may be heard in a few scattered low spots of the state.

MINERALS

The Magnet Cove region of Arkansas is said to have a wider variety of minerals than anywhere else on earth. In the unique assortment there are found more than 42 kinds.

On a statewide basis, in addition to aluminum, gas, oil, and diamonds, the state has glass sand, tripoli, limestone, quartz, novaculite, barite, gypsum, kaolin, iron, manganese, titanium, and columbian.

Above: Greers Ferry Dam on the Little Red River.
Below: Harvesting catfish, one of the state's newest crops.

People Use Their Treasures

TRANSPORTATION AND COMMUNICATION

Floating palaces, paddle-wheel steamboats, made travel on Arkansas' rivers a remarkable experience at one time. Because of the shallowness of many of the rivers, the boats were designed to float in as little water as possible. Someone once remarked that Arkansas steamboats could run anywhere the ground was moist. One of the most elegant and fully equipped boats on the rivers was the *Fort Gibson,* which needed only a foot of water to carry it over the upper reaches of the Arkansas River.

The first steamboat, the *New Orleans,* puffed past the Arkansas banks of the Mississippi in 1811. Little Rock marveled at its first steamboat, the *Eagle,* as early as 1822. The peak of steamboat popularity found a variety of specialized kinds of boats—from the showboats that brought theatrical performances to remote areas to the store boats, some of which were really floating department stores.

Steamboating was a dangerous occupation. Boiler explosions, wrecks, collisions, capsizing, and sinkings were common. The postmaster at Osceola was able to build his cabin using wood and other materials from steamboats that had met disaster.

The day of the steamboat is gone, but river traffic is far larger today than it was before. An unbelievable number of roomy barges can be propelled by unglamorous but hardworking tugboats.

Helena is still an important port.

Many of the rivers, such as the Ouachita, have been made navigable by dams and locks. The development of the Arkansas River has been called one of the greatest engineering construction projects of history. A total of $1,200,000,000 has been spent for power, navigation, and flood control on the Arkansas in a vast program that now permits commercial shipping as far as central Oklahoma, and makes Little Rock a major port.

Before the steamboats, river travel was not so easy. Pirogues, designed on the Indian pattern and hollowed from logs, along with keelboats were the most common means of getting about on the streams, and they required large amounts of human muscle for voyages that would seem unbearably slow today.

Boat travel was easy, however, compared to the hazards and difficulty of going overland.

Early travelers followed the Indian trails on foot. One of the great primitive routes of travel was the Southwest Trail, bypassing hills and swamps and crossing the best fords of the many rivers. When pioneers began to come through the region with wagons, they often had to cut down the trees in their path. About the only lubrication for early wagon wheels was pine tar. During cold weather, fires had to be built under each wheel to soften the tar before the wagons could be made to move in the morning.

When stagecoaches were able to make their way over the rutted roads, they seemed almost luxurious. An advertisement for the line from Little Rock to Fort Smith read: "Passengers will go through by this line in comfortable post-coaches, with excellent stock and careful drivers, in about fifty-four hours."

The famed Butterfield stage route from St. Louis to California ran through Arkansas, and one 1858 traveler has left a revealing account: "I might say our road was steep, rugged, jagged, rough and mountainous . . . and then wish for some more expressive words in the language. The wiry, light, little animals tugged and pulled as if they would tear themselves to pieces, and our heavy wagon bounded along the crags as if it would be shaken to pieces every minute . . .

"As the road winds along the ridges you are afforded most magnificent views of the surrounding hills and valleys . . . and I can only say that our mountain views in the highlands of the Hudson are but children's toys in comparison with these vast works of nature . . . Connecticut hills and roads are mere pimples and sandpaper compared with the Ozark ranges.

"By hard tugging we got up, and with the aid of brakes and drags we got down; and I can assure that we were by no means sorry when that herculean feat was accomplished."

Another passenger, in 1860, had further comment: "Over such a route as this the coaches of the mail company are driven with fearful

rapidity . . . the stage reels from side to side like a storm tossed bark
. . . Yet with all these indications of danger and recklessness, accidents seldom occur . . . The coaches are built expressly with reference to rough service—and none but the most reliable and experienced drivers are placed upon the mountain district. The horses are of the most powerful description to be found, and when once thoroughly trained to the service, perform the laborious run with apparent pleasure and delight.''

By contrast with the rough old trails are the nearly 80,000 miles (about 129,000 kilometers) of modern highway in the state today, including such super roads as Interstates 30 and 40.

The first railroad into Arkansas opened a part of the run between Little Rock and Memphis in 1858.

One of the most interesting stories of railroads in the state is that of the little Diamond Jo line, which as someone has said was founded on rheumatism. Diamond Jo Reynolds, a manufacturer from Chicago, was bounced and jiggled in a stagecoach over the rough road from Malvern on his way to cure his rheumatism at Hot Springs. When the ride was over he groaned, "I've got to come back here some day, but I promise you I'll never ride that way again!" Instead he built the narrow gauge Diamond Jo Railroad, noted for its luxurious furniture of rosewood and mahogany, its upholstery of leather, and draperies of finest velvet. The wealthy and famous passengers such as Gentleman Jim Corbett and Jay Gould often helped the fireman load firewood at the fueling stop at Magnet.

Rail fans from all over the country come to Arkansas today to inspect and enjoy the Reader Railroad, which operates the nation's last remaining regularly scheduled standard gauge steam powered mixed trains. The train is called one of the state's top tourist attractions.

Arkansas' pioneer community, Arkansas Post, was also the location of the first newspaper in the state, the Arkansas *Gazette*. Founded in 1824, it has been called the first newspaper ever published west of the Mississippi. The *Gazette* was later moved to Little Rock, and now is a leading daily.

The Washington *Telegraph* was one of the few Confederate papers

Oil derricks can still be seen in Arkansas, although other minerals are more important.

west of the Mississippi to continue to publish as the war went on. Because of the shortage of paper, it is interesting to note that a number of its issues were printed on wallpaper, which was eagerly read for news of the Confederacy.

EVERYTHING FROM GAS TO DIAMONDS

North America's only diamond mine was operated from 1908 to 1925. Many fine and beautiful stones were taken out, including one weighing 40 carats, worth $8,000. However, most of the diamonds were small, imperfect ones that could be used only for industrial purposes. The mine, near Murfreesboro, now a state park, is open to visitors, who pay a fee to search for diamonds.

Natural gas was first found in Arkansas as early as 1888 but the first well, in a field at Massard Prairie, did not produce gas until 1940.

Since 1925 Arkansas has been one of the nation's eleven leading petroleum producing states. At one time it held sixth place in petroleum, but now is no longer among the leading states. Every effort is made now to conserve the precious petroleum, and the state carefully regulates production for maximum use of the reserves.

More than 96 percent of all the bauxite, or aluminum, ore mined in the United States comes from Arkansas. A large part of this ore is

50

converted into alumina and ingots in Arkansas processing plants.

Several mines in Arkansas produce cinnabar. Until this ore was discovered in Clark and Pike counties, the United States had depended on Spain for most of it. The cinnabar crystals, ruby red in color, are heated until the metal in them condenses, and the vapors are carried off. When cooled, the vapors become mercury or quicksilver, used in thermometers and also in chemical and electrical manufacturing.

Batesville is noted for its beautiful jet-black marble. Coal production in Arkansas is centered at Paris and Greenwood. Manganese and titanium are also mined.

Arkansas produces more barite than any other state. This is used in the making of rubber and paper. The state also ranks first in novaculite whetstones and syenite.

GROWING THINGS

Timber production in Arkansas reached its peak in 1909. In early lumbering, the land was stripped of its trees and left useless. Today, careful production assures the state of growing more timber than it uses. An important source of timber is the small farm where farmers grow trees as one of their regular crops.

Cotton is still king in Arkansas agriculture. Generally the state

A cotton plantation, painted by Henry Lewis.

ranks second or third in the country. Just less than 50 percent of Arkansas' agricultural income comes from cotton. Almost 2 percent of the entire world cotton supply is grown in Mississippi County alone; it is usually listed as one of the principal counties in the United States in agriculture. Near the town of Wilson is one of the world's largest cotton plantations, founded by Robert E. Lee Wilson, who also created the town.

After planting, cotton grows quickly like a tropical plant. The blossoms appear in early June, first white, then turning pink. When the blossoms fall off, a squarish pod called a boll slowly forms. In early August these bolls begin to burst open, much to the delight of visitors who have never seen cotton on the bush. Most people who are not familiar with cotton growing are amazed that puffs of real cotton come bursting out of these hard little balls.

All cotton picking used to be done by hand. Pickers would drag a bag behind them, sometimes 15 or 20 feet (about 5 or 6 meters) long, slung over one shoulder and open at that end to receive the cotton. Pickers were expected to harvest 200 to 300 pounds (about 90 to 136 kilograms) of the light and fluffy material each day. Now most of the picking is done by mechanical picking machines that stride through the fields like metal giants, pulling the cotton from the stalks and throwing it into huge wire bins on trucks. A few small scattered fields are still harvested by hand.

The cotton is carried to the many balers, where the wire-enclosed wagons are often lined up for long distances waiting their turn, until finally the fluffy cotton is compressed into heavy bales.

Rice was introduced into Arkansas in 1904, and today the state usually ranks among the top five in rice production. Stuttgart is labeled as the rice capital of Arkansas.

Soybeans and chicken broilers are the other top money-makers for Arkansas farmers. Arkansas ranks second among all the states in production of broilers.

Tobacco used to be an important crop in the state, but little of it is grown in Arkansas today.

Benton County is noted for its apples, and grape growing also is important in northwest Arkansas. Father Pietro Bandini came to

Arkansas to help a group of Italian people who were having a hard time near Lake Chicot. He bought land in Washington County and moved most of the Italian group there. They brought in slips of fine grapes, and began to cultivate vineyards and make wine. This encouraged others to grow grapes in the region, and the wine making industry still flourishes.

Among Arkansas' most interesting crops are the super watermelons of the Hope region. To grow one, the farmer chooses the best vine and clears all other vines around it. After the watermelons begin to form, he selects just one and removes all others from the vine. Tall plant such as castor beans are planted around the melon to shade it from the sun. Fertilizers are used, and the melon is sometimes even fed a nourishing liquid through the stem.

The resulting melons have reached enormous size and have grown to weights of 195 pounds (about 88 kilograms). Although they look good, they are said not to be very good eating—not very sweet.

By the late 1970s Arkansas' farm income was approaching three billion dollars.

MANUFACTURING

Income from manufacturing in Arkansas is only slightly higher than income from agriculture.

As they were in so many states, trappers were among the earliest men of industry in Arkansas, and animal pelts were one of the earliest important products, as described by Henry Schoolcraft in 1818: "The first object worthy of remark which presented itself on emerging from the forest was the innumerable quantity of deer, bear, and other skins . . . stretched out, and hung up to dry on poles and trees around the house."

Another early product was written about by George Hunter and William Dunbar in 1804: "The hunters count much of their profits from the oil drawn from the bear's fat, which, at New Orleans, is always of ready sale . . . much esteemed for its wholesomeness in cooking, being preferred to butter or hog's lard. It is found to keep

The Ozark Folk Center, in Mountain View, was formed to preserve some of Arkansas' culture. Demonstrations are given on crafts such as woodcarving and quilting.

longer than any other animal oil without becoming rancid, and boiling it, from time to time, upon sweet bay leaves, restores its sweetness.''

One of the earliest true industries was begun by John Hemphill in 1811. He bought a salt spring near Arkadelphia from the Indians, obtained great boiling kettles and evaporating pans, and went into the salt evaporating business.

As a sidelight, it is interesting to note that Little Rock's first industry was a small factory for making hats, begun in 1840.

Among the important types of manufacturing in Arkansas are food products (such as animal feed and soft drinks), furniture, lumber, paper products, petroleum, and instruments.

One of the most interesting small industries of Arkansas is known to many sportsmen around the world. This is the Ben Pearson factory at Pine Bluff, maker of bows and arrows for archery.

Bows and arrows for archery are made in Arkansas

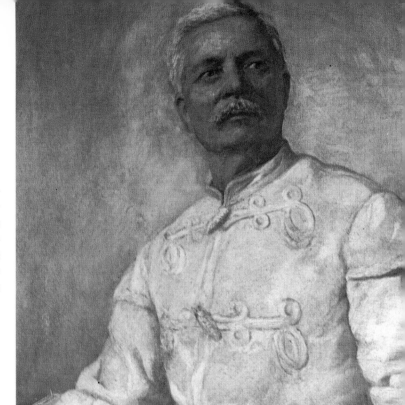

Right: Henry Morton Stanley worked in a country store at Cypress Bend. Below: George Catlin was famous for painting the Indians. Here is his self portrait.

Human Treasures

THE GENTLEMAN AND THE LADY

"These scholorships have done more than any other one thing to increase understanding between peoples of the United States and those of other countries." The speaker was referring to a plan originated by one of Arkansas' most prominent public figures. James William Fulbright was born in 1905. He studied at the University of Arkansas and then completed his education at Oxford in England.

Fulbright served for a time as an attorney in the Department of Justice, then was a law instructor at George Washington University and later at the University of Arkansas. From 1939 to 1941 he served as president of the University of Arkansas.

William Fulbright decided to enter politics and was elected to the House of Representatives from Arkansas in 1942. In 1945 he was chosen as Arkansas' junior United States Senator, and served in the Senate until 1975.

The program that has made his name known around the world was that of the Fulbright Scholarships. The Fulbright-Hays Act established an international educational exchange program. One of the outstanding parts of the plan was to exchange American teachers with those from many countries abroad; the American teacher would take the place of the teacher who came to this country to teach in the American's classroom. Under the program, also, hundreds of scholars were given grants for travel and study abroad.

In 1959, Senator Fulbright was named chairman of the Senate Foreign Relations Committee. He was noted for conflict with President Johnson over foreign affairs, especially the war in Viet Nam.

The traditions of 142 years were broken by an Arkansas woman. Senator T.H. Caraway of Arkansas died in 1931. His wife, Hattie W. Caraway, of Jonesboro, was appointed to succeed him and fill the balance of his term. She became the first woman in United States history to take a seat in the national Senate. Proving that a woman could win such an honor in her own right, Mrs. Caraway was elected to her own full term in the Senate in 1932, and then again in 1938.

OTHER PUBLIC FIGURES

A particularly unusual succession of offices marked the public career of Joseph T. Robinson of Lonoke, known throughout Arkansas as Joe T. Within a few weeks Robinson served as United States Representative, governor of Arkansas, and United States Senator. In 1912 he was serving his fourth term in Congress when he resigned to become governor. Shortly after this, the Arkansas General Assembly, which then chose Senators, elected him to the Senate from Arkansas.

Robinson served in the Senate for twenty-five years until his death in 1937, becoming leader of the Senate Democrats in 1922. He was particularly well known for his fight to aid the poor farmers of the country. Robinson was the unsuccessful candidate for Vice-President of the United States, running with Al Smith in the campaign of 1928.

The first territorial governor of Arkansas was a hero of the War of 1812. When a superior officer asked James I. Miller if he could take an enemy company, he answered, "I'll try, Sir!" He made the capture, and Miller's phrase, "I'll try, Sir!" made him famous.

General Miller started from Pittsburgh in 1819 to make his way downriver by his own private keelboat to his new governor's post in Arkansas. His boat was met everywhere by enthusiastic well-wishers, and the trip took 75 days—only about 10 miles (about 16 kilometers) per day, said one critic. His accomplishments as governor were less notable than his slogan, which was learned by almost every child in school throughout most of the century.

The strange career of Augustus Garland was marked by his successful fight to overcome the disadvantage of Reconstruction. Because he had been a Confederate Congressman, lawyer Garland was forbidden to practice in Federal Courts. He won the famous case before the United States Supreme Court known as *ex parte* Garland and was again permitted in the Federal Courts.

Elected to the United States Senate in 1867, he was refused his seat there. When he was elected governor in 1874, he said the state treasury did not have enough money in it to supply kindling wood for his office fireplace. However, during his term much was done to restore the finances of the state. In 1877 he was again elected to the Senate, and this time won the final triumph by being permitted to take his seat. His public career closed with his service as Attorney General under President Grover Cleveland.

YELL FOR ARKANSAS

One of the best-known military men was born in Little Rock in 1880. This was General of the Army Douglas MacArthur. However, his later career was not intimately connected with his birth state.

Arkansas has produced many other notable military men. Seven Confederate generals came from Helena, alone. Among these were Patrick R. Cleburne and Thomas C. Hindman.

Cleburne enlisted in the Yell Rifles, as a private, and very shortly was made captain and then colonel and finally general. He gained his greatest fame protecting the forces of General Braxton Bragg on his retreat from Lookout Mountain.

Irvin S. Cobb wrote a dramatic account of his death: "Pat Cleburne died on one of the bloodiest battlefields of Christendom in his stocking feet because, as he rode into battle that morning he saw one of his Irish boys from Little Rock tramping barefoot over the frozen furrows of a wintry cornfield and leaving tracks of blood behind him. So he drew off his boots and bade the soldier put them on, and fifteen minutes later he went to his God in his stocking feet. Raleigh laid down his coat before Good Queen Bess, and has been immortalized for his chivalry, but I think a more courtly deed was that of the gallant Irishman Pat Cleburne."

Hindman and Cleburne worked caring for victims of a yellow fever epidemic at Helena and became very good friends. As one writer described him, Hindman was "almost fresh from the blood-stained fields of Mexico, where he had been promoted for valorous conduct from a private to a first lieutenant . . . He regarded Arkansas as an empire of which he should be emperor. At this time fire ran through all his veins and dynamite through his brains."

Hindman took charge of the defenses of the Confederate state of Arkansas in 1862, beginning with the Battle of Prairie Grove. Later he served the Confederate cause in eastern battles. When the Confederate surrender came, Hindman would not surrender and managed to make his escape across the border to Mexico.

After about a year he returned to Helena, where his strange death took place in 1868. As he leaned over his mother's bed, some unknown person shot him. Before he died he managed to murmur, according to his neighbors, "I do not know who killed me; but I can say, whoever it was, I forgive him."

An Arkansas hero of three wars, as well as a romantic figure in early Arkansas politics, was Colonel Archibald Yell. He served under Andrew Jackson in both the War of 1812, at the Battle of New Orleans, and in the Seminole War. Later he led a force of Arkansas troops in the Mexican War and died at Buena Vista.

He had come to Arkansas as a Federal Judge for the western region, appointed by then President Jackson, and settled at Fayetteville. After Arkansas became a state, Yell became the first Congressman from the new state. He ran for governor and was elected in 1844. The story is told that in a very lively campaign, he paid a visit to a little town called Shawneetown. Tradition has it that he offered the people of the town $50 if they would change the name of the village to Yellville; they did, and the town has been named for the well-known political figure ever since.

CREATIVE PEOPLE

One of the earliest literary figures of Arkansas was Albert Pike, who came from Boston to Van Buren in 1832, and had a picturesque career as poet, newspaperman, explorer, Indian commissioner, and general. Some of his poems gained attention in such renowned publications as *Blackwoods Magazine* of Scotland. Some experts say that one of his poems gave Edgar Allan Poe the idea for his poem *The Raven.* Among other activities in his varied career, Pike led a Confederate troop of Cherokee Indians, fought at least one duel, and became one of the world's best-known authorities on Masonry. Before his death he finished a massive writing project on the subject of Masonry. Another well-known Arkansas poet was John Gould Fletcher.

An Arkansas novelist of wide renown was Alice French of Clover Bend, who used the professional name of Octave Thanet. At Clover Bend she gathered the background information for her novels *By Inheritance* and *Otto the Knight*.

Many homespun humorists were developed in Arkansas, basing their humor on the simple life around them and often distorting their neighbors beyond all recognition. One of the most widely read of these was Opie Read of Conway. One of his stories told of his going to the town well to get a bucket of water. Several friends joined him, passed the bucket around for drinks and told the gossip of the day. At last Read drawled, "Well, fellows, I don't want to hurry you, but the printing office is on fire, and I just came down for a bucket of water to put the fire out."

Colonel Sandford D. (Sandy) Faulkner is given credit for creating the lively dance tune and the fanciful conversation that have come to be known as the *Arkansaw Traveler*. The first part of this has already been referred to. As the frustrated traveler kept on talking to the squatter without getting any offer of hospitality, he finally said, "What are you playing that tune over so often for?" Squatter: "Only heard it yisterday. 'Fraid I'll forget it." Traveler: "Why don't you play the second part of it?" Squatter: "It ain't got no second part." Traveler: "Give me the fiddle."

After tuning the fiddle, the Traveler swept into the second part. The Squatter jumped to his feet and into a lively dance; the hound dog raised his head and pounded his tail; the old woman came out and broke into a seldom seen smile.

When he was exhausted the Squatter stopped dancing and wheezed, "Come in, stranger. Take a half a dozen cheers and sot down. Sal, stir yourself round like a six-horse team in a mud hole. Go round in the holler, whar I killed that buck this mornin', cut off some of the best pieces and fotch it and cook it for me and this gentleman directly. Raise up the board under the head of the bed

The Arkansas Traveler, *a lithograph by John H. Bufford about 1871.*

and git the old black jug I hid and give us some whiskey; I know thar's some left yet. Dick, carry the gentleman's hoss around under the shed, give him some fodder and corn, as much as he kin eat . . . Stranger . . . stay as long as you please, and I'll give you plenty to eat and drink. Play away, stranger, you kin sleep on the dry spot tonight!''

Arkansas' most famous picture was done by Edward Payson Washburn to show the *Arkansaw Traveler.* This painting shows the Squatter sitting on a keg holding his fiddle and the handsomely dressed Traveler arguing unsuccessfully with him. Copies of the picture were widely distributed around the world on everything from calendars to magazines. Washburn was working on a sequel to the picture, to be called *Turn of the Tune,* when he died. He was only 28 years old.

Some of the most interesting paintings done in Arkansas were those of famed Indian painter George Catlin, who found many of his subjects at Fort Smith. Perhaps the first Arkansas woman artist to be given nationwide attention was Jennie Deloney Rice-Meyrowitz,

62

native of Washington, Arkansas. The first professional artist to live in Arkansas was John Henry Byrd.

Arkansas' William Grant Still, composer of *Afro-American Symphony,* is one of the country's better-known composers. Mary McCormic, native of Belleville, gained fame as an operatic singer.

SUCH INTERESTING PEOPLE

Miss Willie K. Hocker of Pine Bluff designed Arkansas' state flag, adopted in 1913. Miss Hocker's plan called for a white diamond in the center of a red field, with a border of blue around the white diamond. In the blue border are 25 stars, indicating the 25th state. In the white diamond are three large blue stars to represent the three nations of Spain, France, and the United States, of which Arkansas has been a part. They also show that Arkansas was the third state created from the Louisiana Territory. The large star above the word "Arkansas" recalls the Confederacy. The diamond itself indicates that Arkansas is the only diamond producing state.

The history of the state is also symbolized in the riddle carved on the tombstone of John Patterson, often claimed to be the first white child born in present-day Arkansas. It reads:

I was born in a Kingdom (Spain)

Raised in an Empire (France)

Attained manhood in a Territory

Am now a citizen of a State

And have never been 100 miles from where I now live.

A much more traveled resident was Captain B.L.E. Bonneville, one of the most famed explorers of the West. He helped to select the site of Fort Smith, was a commandant there, and when his career was over he retired to Fort Smith.

Another early figure was James Black of Washington. He is thought to have been the cutlery maker who followed James Bowie's design to make the first of the renowned Bowie knives. Black said he improved the design and made many of them in his blacksmith shop at Washington. He claimed to test each one by whittling on solid hickory with the knife for a half hour and then using it to shave with.

Dr. Benjamin Bugg of Blytheville claimed to have the longest beard in the world. He was terribly proud of the whiskers that swept down from his chin. However, he went to the World's Columbian Exposition at Chicago in 1893 and saw a beard that was longer than his. He came home and immediately cut off his noted trademark.

Charles McDermott of Dermott was an early experimenter with flying machines. He applied for a number of patents in the field of aviation and became known as Flying Machine Charlie. A real flier was Mrs. Louise McPhetridge Thaden. In 1936 she received the famed Harmon Trophy for being the outstanding woman flier of the country.

An unusual story of success belongs to William Hope Harvey. In 1894 he wrote a book on how to solve the nation's money problems. It became one of the all-time best sellers, with more than a million copies sold. Harvey became an adviser to William Jennings Bryan, and it is thought he had much to do with Bryan's *Cross of Gold* speech. He denounced the brokers of Wall Street and retired to Monte Ne; after the financial crash of 1929, which he had predicted, Harvey came out of retirement, organized the Liberty Party and ran for President in 1932 against Herbert Hoover and Franklin D. Roosevelt.

Harvey's later life was spent in a strange plan to build a great pyramid, like those of Egypt, at Monte Ne, in which relics of American civilization could be preserved for ages, but he died before it could be finished.

Three very different storekeepers played their part in Arkansas. Benjamin Foy set up his store near present West Memphis and began the town of Hopefield, one of the earliest in Arkansas. One writer said of Foy that he "appears to have possessed a far more extensive and correct knowledge of the country than any other man in it." Another writer mentioned "Mr. Foy's handsome settlement and good frame house."

The story is told that Matthew F. Rainey's wagon broke down as he was traveling in 1843. Because he could not go on, he decided to sell some of his possessions. The neighborhood farmers were so eager to purchase them that he decided to get more goods and open a store. A community formed around his store, and he called it El Dorado.

Arkansas' most famous storeman, however, probably was Henry Morton Stanley. During a relaxed period of his adventurous life, Stanley dispensed calico and groceries in the country store of Louis Altshul at Cypress Bend on the Arkansas River. Later Stanley wandered all over the globe as a reporter and explorer, especially in the American West and later in Africa. He gained his greatest fame by finding Dr. Livingstone in Africa. Stanley later lived in England and was knighted by the queen.

A number of notable Indians have called Arkansas home. One of the best-known of all time was Sequoya, known as George Guess, the Cherokee scholar, who created the written language of his people. He came to Arkansas with a group of the Cherokee after the Treaty of 1817.

Cherokee Chief Takatoka created a plan to bring together as many Indians as possible in a peaceful confederation of the West. He hoped that a strong Indian nation would be able to keep peace with the wild western groups and also with the European settlers. He traveled with great energy to promote his dream but died in 1824 before his Indian nation could be brought into being.

Another Indian leader was Chief Black Fox. The interesting story is told that Robert Crittenden, secretary of Arkansas Territory, met with a group of Indians to talk about their giving up still more of their treaty land. Black Fox sat next to Crittenden on a log. Several times he asked Crittenden to move over on the log to give him a little more room. Soon the indignant Crittenden replied that if he moved any farther he would fall off the log. Black Fox then pointed out: "That is the way with us. Our Great Father has moved us from place to place until we can get no farther."

One of the most highly regarded of the Quapaw chiefs was Chief Sarasen. Always a friend of the Europeans, at one time he rescued two white children kidnapped by an enemy group. Sarasen was one of the many Indian leaders who lived to a surprising old age. He died in 1832, at the age of 97.

Teaching and Learning

There are 13 four-year colleges in the state of Arkansas. Philander Smith College at Little Rock, founded in 1868, is the oldest institution of higher education now operating in the state.

Arkansas Industrial University was opened at Fayetteville in 1872 as one of the Land Grant colleges under the Morrill Act of 1862. This act gave land to colleges established for the benefit of agriculture and mechanical arts. The first graduating class in 1876 had five men and four women. In 1899 the name was changed to the University of Arkansas.

Near the Fayetteville campus is the Agricultural Experiment Station of the university. Here experiments are carried on to see what are the best crops for the state. Branches of the Experimental Station are operated at Batesville for livestock and forestry, for rice at Stuttgart, and for truck and fruit crops at Hope.

The University of Arkansas also operates a medical branch at Little Rock (established in 1879), a Graduate Institute of Technology, also at Little Rock, and other branches.

Other institutions supported by the state are Henderson State University, Arkadelphia; University of Central Arkansas, Conway; Arkansas State University; Arkansas Southern University, Magnolia; and Arkansas Polytechnic College, Russellville.

Private colleges include Ouachita Baptist University, Arkadelphia; Arkansas College, Batesville; College of the Ozarks, Clarksville; Hendrix College, Conway; Harding College, Searcy; and John Brown University and Siloam Springs at Walnut Ridge.

The research facilities of the state are growing rapidly. Much of the research work is being done at the various installations of the University of Arkansas. A $25,000,000 experimental nuclear reactor near Fayetteville is one of the principal research instruments of the state.

Arkansas is one of the leaders in adopting television for educa-

Opposite: An outdoor theater at the University of Arkansas.

Right: Breedlove Fine Arts Building, Westark Community College in Fort Smith. Below: The University of Arkansas' razorbacks have brought fame to the state.

tional uses. The tower of KATV, Little Rock, the world's second tallest man-made structure, is used to beam educational programs across the state. It is said to be among the finest educational television facilities in the world.

Conway is the home of the internationally known Children's Colony, a state facility for treating retarded children. It has been called the best of its kind in North America and has been visited by medical authorities from several foreign countries.

To help people train for jobs and to assist industry to find capable workers, vocational-technical schools are available in every region of the state.

Autumn in Arkansas.

Enchantment of Arkansas

Many millions of out-of-state visitors come to Arkansas yearly to see the varied attractions of the state. They come in the spring when the slopes are gleaming with the white bloom of dogwood, and wild roses carpet the forest floor; they come when blue waves lap at the edges of dark green forests and the splash of fish tempt fishermen to float lazily down the streams in search of them; they come when autumn burnishes the countryside with splashes of yellow, orange, and crimson and squawking ducks almost black out the sun; they come in winter when the warm waters of the springs offer relief to tired bodies, aching from the northern cold.

They come to the state parks where history and recreation combine, to the Civil War battlefield parks and the national cemeteries to pay tribute to the dead, to the reproductions and restorations of storied buildings and places, to the museums, symphonies, and other attractions of the cities. They come to experience for themselves what so many already know as the enchantment of Arkansas.

CAPITAL OF CAPITOLS

Little Rock claims to be the only city in the country where three state capitols are still standing. If the walls of those three buildings could talk they would tell much of the history of the state.

The oldest of the three is the territorial capitol. Built in 1820 and remodeled in 1834, it is constructed of large hand-hewn oak logs covered with handbeaded cypress siding. All the ceiling beams, both upstairs and down, have the same beaded finish.

When it was decided to restore this old capitol, the building was found in such good condition that little more than removing an accumulation of many old coats of paint and the various additions was needed to bring the building back almost to its original state.

A number of old buildings in the territorial capitol block are also being restored, making a whole community as it looked in territorial days. The group includes the home and office of William E.

Woodruff, founder of the Arkansas *Gazette,* oldest newspaper west of the Mississippi, and the Conway house, home of Elias N. Conway, who was a governor of the state. His brother, James S. Conway, was the first governor of the state.

Many people of interest, including Washington Irving, James Audubon, Sam Houston, and Davy Crockett, were entertained in the homes of the restoration area.

The Noland house, offices, stables, milk house, separate kitchens, and herb gardens are other features of the restoration, which was the inspiration of Mrs. J. Fairfax Loughborough. The legislature made the restoration possible beginning in 1939, and a state commission was formed to supervise it, under the direction of Mrs. Loughborough, who served until her death in 1963. The buildings are furnished with authentic pieces of the times.

From 1836 to 1910 the state government was carried on in the Old State House, acclaimed as one of the finest examples of antebellum architecture in the South. The building was built on the site of an ancient Indian burial ground; its beautiful columned porch with a view of the Arkansas River, the striking twin spiral stairways, multiple arched hallways, and chandeliered rooms make it a building of distinction. It was restored by the state beginning in 1947.

Here the secession convention and four constitutional conventions were held; here a pioneer speaker of the House of Representatives once stabbed to death a fellow legislator in an argument over the bounty on wolf scalps; here, on a wager, it is said that leading Arkansas men tried to ride their horses up the spiral stairs. Here the first arguments of the Brooks-Baxter War took place. The old cannon, Lady Baxter, still stands guard on the front lawn as a memento of this argument.

The building houses the Arkansas History Commission, with a fine collection of archives. The currency room displays the Harry B. Solmson collection of Confederate and Southern state currency, considered the finest of its kind in the world.

The museum in the building houses a collection of the original inaugural gowns of Arkansas' first ladies and rooms furnished in many different periods.

*The State
Capitol
Building*

The present capitol building was designed by the famous architect of capitols Cass Gilbert, and it is said to be a reproduction on a smaller scale of the Capitol at Washington.

Although the foundations were begun as early as 1899, nothing was done to continue the work. George W. Donaghey ran for governor in 1909 on a platform of finishing the capitol; he was elected, and two years later the legislature managed to meet in the building. The cornerstone was laid November 27, 1900, and the building was entirely completed in 1915. Most of the stone was Batesville marble. To the west of the capitol are more recent buildings, housing various departments of government.

Arkansas' first official governor's mansion was completed in January, 1950, after a two-year construction period. The mansion, a Georgian Colonial type, is located on over 6 acres (about 7 hectares) of grounds, and guest houses flank the mansion on each side. The buildings are constructed of age-mellowed, oversized brick from old state properties.

Little Rock recalls one of her most famous sons, General of the Army Douglas MacArthur, in MacArthur Park. The general was born in the arsenal building there, which once was the home of army officers and their wives. The arsenal building is now the home of the Little Rock Museum of Science and Natural History. The MacArthur bedroom is displayed there. The museum is especially known for its collection of pattern glass.

Also in MacArthur Park is the striking Fine Arts Center. The Arts Center operates 27 divisions in various parts of the state, as well as one in Greenville, Mississippi. The Center at Little Rock includes

The old arsenal building, where General MacArthur was born.

five exhibition galleries and a theater. Its Artmobile, a miniature gallery on wheels, travels to all parts of the state with art displays.

The hut of William Lewis, not tall enough to stand in, in 1812 was the first European-type building in Little Rock, and he scattered a handful of pumpkin seeds around the building in order to make his claim valid by improving the land.

The town grew slowly; in 1834 an Englishman named George Featherstonhaugh made a very wrong prediction: "The town of Little Rock is surrounded by extremely poor land and from a variety of concurring causes can never be very populous. [But] in virtue of it being the seat of government, it may in time become a respectable small town, have good seminaries of education . . . and afford agreeable society."

When Davy Crockett visited Little Rock in 1834, on his way to Texas, the citizens held a shooting contest and celebrated with a bear cub, wild turkey, and venison banquet. The people tried to persuade Crockett to stay. He said he would not be able to, but "If I could rest anywhere it would be in Arkansaw, where the men are of the real half-horse, half-alligator breed such as grow nowhere else on the face of the universal earth but just around the backbone of North America."

Modern Little Rock, with its metropolitan population of more than 350,000, its rings of superhighways, mushrooming skyscrapers, and rapidly advancing industry is a far cry from those pioneer days that are not much more than a hundred years away.

LOW COUNTRY

Dominating the low country of Arkansas, of course, is the mighty Father of Waters, the Mississippi. One of the most scenic roads in the world, the Great River Road, follows the river as closely as possible and gives intriguing glimpses of the river country.

At Blytheville, in October, there is the annual National Cotton Picking Contest. Here nimble fingered contestants vie for top honors in harvesting Arkansas' number one crop.

Near Manila is Herman Davis State Park, honoring Arkansas' greatest hero of World War I.

Wilson, in its entirety, is part of the world's largest cotton plantation. In Wilson is the ultramodern Hampson Museum, displaying the choicest of 40,000 items left by the prehistoric peoples.

West Memphis is the eastern gateway into Arkansas, where a special attraction is the greyhound racing. In 1930 the population of West Memphis was only 1,000; since that time it has multiplied more than 15 times.

Forrest City was named for Confederate General Nathan Bedford Forrest. General Forrest took the contract to lay a railroad over Crowley's Ridge, on which the city stands.

One of the most interesting prehistoric relics in the state is the enormous deposit of oyster shells tossed out, over the centuries, by ancient peoples who lived there. It is estimated to contain 7,000,000 cubic yards (about 5,350,000 cubic meters) of shells—representing a lot of prehistoric eating.

The old river port of Helena is a thriving city, still an important seaport. It is filled with historic houses such as the Horner home, center of the Battle of Helena, with rifle bullets and cannon balls still imbedded on its walls.

On June 7, 1862, St. Charles made its name in military history. Union riverboats were trying to go up the Mississippi. A Confederate cannon sent one cannonball through a porthole of the *Mound City;* the steam pipes were smashed and 150 troops were killed. This has been called the most destructive single shot of the war.

Arkansas Post, once the capital with 3,500 people, at present is almost a ghost town. However, the historic old community is now Arkansas Post National Monument, recalling the adventure, romance, and violent drama of the post's turbulent past. An interesting museum helps to recall the stirring events that took place there.

Dumas gained fame in a strange way—through the once widely popular ragtime tune *I'm a Ding Dong Daddy from Dumas.*

Near Arkansas City once stood the town of Napoleon, engulfed and destroyed by a flood, as told by Mark Twain: "It was an astonishing thing to see the Mississippi rolling between unpeopled shores and straight over the spot where I used to see a good big self-complacent town twenty years ago. Town that was county-seat of a great and important county; town with a big United States marine hospital; . . . a town no more—swallowed up, vanished, gone to feed the fishes; nothing left but a fragment of a shanty and a crumbling brick chimney.''

Lake Village has erected a memorial to Charles A. Lindbergh, which recalls the fact that he made his first night flight there in April, 1923.

The Lake Chicot region was made notorious by the outlaw band of about 1,000 pirates who followed John Murrell, whose fortress headquarters stood on Stuart's Island. This vicious mob pirated river boats, made counterfeit currency, robbed stores, mails, and banks and kidnapped slaves, among their other outrages, ranging over many states. Finally Murrell was captured, and citizens of the Lake Chicot region destroyed his headquarters, leaving not a trace.

Junction City is one of the several communities divided between two states.

El Dorado led a quiet existence until oil was found; in the frantic rush that followed, 460 producing wells were brought in, making the

This cracking tower converts crude oil into petroleum based products.

town live up to its name. Today the Lion Oil Company has a large refinery there. The Oil Belt Golf Tournament is one of the largest in the south for amateurs.

Near Calion is historic Champagnolle Landing, one of the earliest towns in the state. Here tradition says Daniel Boone frequently camped on his wanderings.

Camden is an industrial city with International Paper, Camden Furniture, and Camark Pottery among its leading firms.

Pine Bluff claims it fired a shot earlier in 1861 than the ones at Fort Sumter that started the Civil War. Joseph Bonne founded Pine Bluff in 1819 as a trading post with the friendly Quapaw Indians. Part of his success may have been because he was half Quapaw. Today the Pine Bluff Arsenal is a $265,000,000 government installation. The Southwestern Railroad has large shops at Pine Bluff.

HIGHER GROUND

Possibly the most famous of all two-state cities in the country is Texarkana. It appears to be one city, but right down the middle of State Line Avenue is the imaginary line, the boundary that separates Arkansas from Texas. The Federal Building and Post Office lies half on one side, half on the other, and the Union Station also rests in both states.

The story is told that Colonel Gus Knobel had surveyed the area for a railroad; when he came to the state line he scrawled on a board "Tex-Ark-Ana." When he nailed the board to a tree he declared, "This is the name of the town that will be built here." The word is taken not only from Arkansas and Texas but the last syllable, "ana," is a tribute to nearby Louisiana.

Washington, which served as the state capital from 1863 to 1865, is described as a living museum with its aging houses and memories of past days. A young scientist, Nathan Douglas Smith, made some of the earliest scientific studies and observations of the weather in his years at Washington.

Near Emmet is Arkla Village, a re-created pioneer town typical of southwest Arkansas, with authentic buggy works, blacksmith shop, general store, and a saloon that serves nothing stronger than sarsaparilla.

One of the most unique and exciting tourist attractions anywhere is found at Murfreesboro. Here is the Crater of Diamonds, once the continent's only diamond mine. Now the crater is open to visitors who pay a fee and have the thrill of hoping they may scrape up from the damp black soil a valuable gem. This is no impossible dream. Since the crater has been open to visitors, they have picked up more than 500 diamonds, some of very good size and considerable value. The visitor may keep any stone under five carats but must pay a percentage to the state for any diamond over that weight.

Other much admired glittering stones are found at Crystal Mountain near Mt. Ida. Quartz crystals are chipped from Monte Cristo Mines and sold in nearby roadside stands.

No one has ever been quite sure if Mt. Ida is the Mount Idy made famous by television humorist Charlie Weaver.

Another community given national publicity by entertainers was Pine Ridge. Radio comedians Lum and Abner used background material from the town of Waters, Arkansas. They called their town Pine Ridge, and eventually the Arkansas town took that name to capitalize on the publicity.

At historic Fort Smith famed and feared Judge Parker held his court every day except Sundays and Christmas. His courtroom and gallows have been re-created to remind visitors of the strict but just man who brought law and order to the frontier.

The first fort can no longer be seen but a building of the second fort, begun in 1838, now houses a museum of pioneer items and war relics.

W.J. Weaver wrote a description of Fort Smith at that time: "On the bank fronting the river were about 15 buildings, reaching over two blocks from the avenue (Garrison Avenue) to Captain Du Val's store below. There was no wharf at the landing in front of the town, nothing but a side cut road down to the edge of the water. Upon the bank in front of Commercial Row . . . [there were] ox wagons, a stir of trade . . . mounted officers charging about on spirited horses, many Indians with baskets and jugs, a few soldiers from the camp, and laborers and mechanics going to and from their work on the new stone fort."

Today Fort Smith is not only the second largest city but also the principal manufacturing center of Arkansas, humming with the activities of more than 200 factories, making products ranging from Dixie cups to refrigerators. There are over 100 different products produced in the city.

During World War II Fort Chaffee was an important training place for armored divisions. Now it is used as headquarters for the 29th Corps of the Army Reserve.

Looking down over the Poteau River is the National Cemetery, final resting place for both Confederate and Union dead. In the cemetery are such poignant markings as "8 Confederate Soldiers," still more of that great number of war dead whose identities are "unknown."

Between Mountainburg and Winslow is the Albert Pike Museum, housed in the log schoolroom where Pike taught in 1832. Some of the belongings of Pike and other items are in the museum. The famed Henderson Early American Glassware Collection of more than 5,000 pieces, once housed here, has been moved to the University of Arkansas.

Fayetteville is an Ozark resort center renowned for its apples and strawberries as well as its scenery, which is particularly colorful in spring and fall.

On the University of Arkansas 140-acre (about 57 hectares) campus at Fayetteville are many interesting buildings. Illinois residents should find the Administration Building of the university familiar. It was modeled after Old Main at the University of Illinois. Its great towers rise 150 feet (about 46 meters) to become visible over a large area.

Contrasting with the Administration Building is the very modern Fine Arts Center, which has a theater, library, concert hall, and exhibition gallery where showings of art are almost constant.

One of the unique festivals in the country is the Medieval Crossbow Pageant held at Huntsville, the only one of its kind. When

Tudor England lives again, there is precision shooting by some of America's best crossbowmen. There is also a princess and her court. The young "crossbowettes" give exhibitions of their ability with the crossbow. The noted crossbow deer hunt immediately follows the pageant.

Raising of poultry is the principal industry of the Springdale region, but the city is in the center of the grape area, and the Welch Grape Juice Company is located there. The Tontitown Grape Festival is a fast-moving annual event. The able craftsmen of the region exhibit their art at the Ozark Arts and Crafts Fair held each year in Springdale.

Inundated by Beaver Lake are the reminders of the strange pyramid of American culture which William Hope Harvey had started to build before his death. Here also was Harvey's tomb, which has been removed.

Sulphur Springs is a popular health resort. The entire Benton County region is noted for its apple blossoms and several towns of the area sponsor annual apple blossom tours to show off the best.

One of the most fascinating communities of America is Eureka Springs in the heart of the Ozarks. Set on the sides of the valley, the town has one street that is never crossed by another as it wanders crazily up and down the slope, winding in and out, finally passing all the houses and places of business—all set at widely different levels. The many springs give the town its name, and several caves open right onto the street.

Although it is seven stories tall, every floor of the Basin Park Hotel is at ground level. Each floor opens onto the hill at a different height. Worshipers at St. Elizabeth's Church enter the second floor sanctuary by way of the steeple.

Carrie Nation was planning to start a school at Eureka Springs to train her prohibitionist followers, and Hatchet Hall may still be seen there; she gave her last prohibition speech in Eureka Springs but died before the school could be started.

The Bracken Ridge Museum at Eureka Springs specializes in dolls, displaying more than 1,000 of them.

On Magnetic Mountain near Eureka Springs is the giant statue of

Christ of the Ozarks, said to be the only mammoth statue of Christ in North America.

All of these and other attractions, including several lakes, and huge Pivot Rock, balancing on a bottom fifteen times smaller than its top, bring more than 200,000 tourists to Eureka Springs each year. In October, tourists come for the annual Ozark Folk Festival.

At Berryville is the museum housing the famous Saunders collection of more than 1,000 guns, including a Chinese pistol 500 years old. Guns owned by Jesse James, Wild Bill Hickok, Pancho Villa, and others are featured. Near Berryville is Mystery Cave, 100 feet (about 30 meters) underground and teeming with trout.

One of the main attractions of the Ozark region is float fishing. Currents of the river carry the boat past beautiful scenery on a leisurely trip that is within fly rod's reach of some of the country's fightingest fish. Float fishing in Arkansas is said to have reached its highest state of development on such streams as the Current, Eleven Point, Caddo, Strawberry, Black, Kings, War Eagle, Saline, Cossatot, and Ouachita rivers. Nowhere is the illusion of getting away from it all so completely sustained as on an Arkansas float trip.

Two famous highways cut through the Ozarks: one is the Ozark Frontier Trail; the other is famed State Highway 7, ranked by many experts to be among the world's ten most scenic roads, riding the valleys and the crests of the Ozarks, long famous in story and fable for their rugged and friendly people and their picturesque loveliness.

Harrison, Jasper, and Russellville are three Route 7 communities. At Harrison is the Bryant Art Center, known as one of the best in a community of its size. Petit Jean Mountain and State Park was named for a young woman who, according to legend, secretly accompanied a French expedition across the Atlantic and up the Arkansas River to be near her sweetheart, who commanded the ship. She became ill and died and is supposed to have been buried on the top of the mountain that bears her name.

It is strange to think that a grove of cedar trees near Plumerville is all that remains to show the site of Cadron, and yet this town at one time was a rival of Little Rock.

*Above: Hot Springs.
Left: Penn Castle,
built in 1878, in
Eureka Springs, is
an exact replica of
an old English home.*

WHERE IT'S GOOD TO BE IN HOT WATER

The fierce Osage and the brave Quapaw warriors suddenly and unexpectedly came face to face, but there was no battle. Instead the two early inhabitants of Arkansas merely lay down in the hot mud with deep sighs of relief. To the Indians this was sacred ground where the healing waters of the Great Spirit gushed forth. All groups were permitted to use it freely, and there were no conflicts. The lame and afflicted often made their way to the place from very far away.

Fishing is both a sport and an industry in Arkansas.

*The Ozark
Mountains*

Today thousands of people still visit the place to soak away their pains and afflictions. It is no longer known as holy ground but as Hot Springs National Park.

Thomas Nuttall described it in 1819: "The principal fountain, issuing from amidst huge masses of black rocks . . . has a stream of near a foot (about 30 centimeters) in diameter at its orifice, and hot enough to boil eggs or fish; a steam arises from it as from water in a state of ebullition, attended with a considerable discharge of bubbles. It is only after mixing with the cool water of a brook, at some distance from this spring, that it becomes of a temperature in which it is possible to bathe."

No one is quite sure why the 47 hot springs flow from the base of Hot Springs Mountain with an average temperature of 143 degrees Fahrenheit (61.7 degrees Celsius). The most logical explanation is that surface water seeps into the ground until it meets heated rocks or hot gasses that make it boil; then it finally flows steaming out through faults in the rock. Others say that water in rocks far below the surface is heated by the earth's fires until it is forced out to the surface.

Whatever the explanation, the waters have been valued since prehistoric times for their healing qualities. About a million gallons of water flows each day; this is collected in reservoirs and piped to the elegant bathhouses of Bathhouse Row, all privately owned on land leased from the government. Two of the springs have been kept in their natural state so that visitors may see what they once were like. A 12-foot-wide (about 3.7 meters) sidewalk in front of the bathhouses covers Hot Springs Creek, which carries the waters of many other cold springs as well as the waste waters from the hot springs. Beautiful Bathhouse Row is lined with stately magnolias and showy holly trees.

Sophisticated Hot Springs city is one of the country's leading tourist communities. A striking new convention center and audi-

The skyline of Little Rock.

Hot Springs in Ouachita Mountains.

torium of ultra-modern design, championship golf courses, Oaklawn race track, fine stores, elegant hotels, motels, and restaurants—all are attractions in addition to the baths.

The Administration Building of the National Park has a fine museum that explains the thermal springs, the early history of the region, and the minerals, insects, and timber of the region.

The observation tower on Hot Springs Mountain and several other outlooks above the city offer some of the country's outstanding scenic views. Hot Springs city is in the heart of the beautiful Ouachita Mountain region, named for the Ouachita Indians.

According to some authorities, the name Ouachita means People of the Clear Sparkling Waters.

Such sparkling waters are found in abundance in the Ouachitas. Hot Springs is surrounded by a world-famed chain of lakes created by damming the Ouachita River at three different points.

With so many attractions, it is not surprising that more than a million people a year visit the Hot Springs region, possibly searching for their own personal kind of revival of spirit that so many have found in Arkansas.

Handy Reference Section

Instant Facts

Became the 25th state, June 15, 1836
Capital—Little Rock, founded 1812
State Motto—*Regnat Populus* (The People Rule)
Nickname—Land of Opportunity
State bird—Mockingbird
State flower—Apple blossom
State stone—Diamond
State tree—Pine
State song—*Arkansas,* words and music by Eva Ware Barnett
Area—53,104 square miles (137,539 square kilometers)
Greatest length (north to south)—275 miles (443 kilometers)
Greatest width (east to west)—240 miles (386 kilometers)
Highest point—2,753 feet (839 meters), Mount Magazine
Lowest point—55 feet (17 meters), southeast corner
Geographic center—Pulaski, 12 miles (19 kilometers) northwest of Little
  Rock
Number of counties—75
Population—2,118,000 (1980 projection)
Population Density—39.88 per square mile (15.39 per square kilometer),
  1980 projection
Rank in Density—32nd
Birthrate—16.7 per 1,000 people
Physicians per 100,000 population—93

Principal cities—	
Little Rock	141,143 (1975 est.)
Fort Smith	62,808 (1970 census)
North Little Rock	60,040
Pine Bluff	57,389
Hot Springs	35,631
Fayetteville	31,915
Jonesboro	28,962
West Memphis	28,236
El Dorado	25,283

You Have a Date with History

1541—Hernando de Soto penetrates Arkansas
1673—Marquette and Jolliet visit

1682—Sieur de la Salle visits region
1686—Arkansas Post founded, first settlement in lower Louisiana
1718—John Law begins Mississippi Company colonization
1722—Bernard de La Harpe traverses Arkansas River
1763—France transfers Louisiana to Spain
1797—Helena founded
1800—Spain gives Louisiana back to France
1808—First Cherokee migrate to region
1812—Little Rock founded
1817—Fort Smith post established
1819—Arkansas Territory established
1821—Capital moved to Little Rock
1836—Statehood
1858—First railroad operates
1860—First telegraph line in Arkansas
1861—Arkansas secedes
1862—Battles of Pea Ridge and Prairie Grove
1863—Little Rock captured by Federal troops
1864—New state government set up at Little Rock
1865—War ends
1868—Readmitted to Union
1872—University of Arkansas opens
1874—Brooks-Baxter War
1875—Judge Isaac Parker brings law to Fort Smith
1887—Bauxite discovered
1904—Rice introduced
1906—Diamonds discovered
1913—Great fire at Hot Springs; state flag adopted
1917—World War I begins in which 63,632 from Arkasas serve
1919—Discovery well heralds first state oil, Stephens
1921—Oil discovered at El Dorado
1927—Strong wrecked by tornado; severe floods
1930—Extreme drought
1932—Arkansas gives nation first woman Senator, Hattie W. Caraway
1941—World War II begins in which more than 200,000 from Arkansas
        see service
1957—President Eisenhower intervenes at Central High School
1963—General Assembly makes *Arkansas* state's official song
1965—General Assembly reapportioned to comply with ruling of United
        States Supreme Court
1967—Winthrop Rockefeller becomes first Republican Governor since
        Reconstruction
1970—McClellan-Kerr Arkansas River Navigation System opens
        Arkansas River to barge traffic across the state
1977—Hollabaugh historical art collection given to state

Annual Events

March—National Blue Tick Coon Dog Trials, Paragould
March-April—Easter Sunrise Service, Hot Springs
April—Trail of the Dogwoods, Northern Arkansas
April—Ozark Foothills Handicraft and Guild Show, Mountain View
April-May—Grand Prairie Grand Prix (Sports Cars), Stuttgart
May—Pioneer Day, Melborne
May—Northwest Arkansas Regional Poultry Festival, Springdale
May—National Professional Golf Assn. Tournament, Hot Springs
May—Sidewalk Art Show, Magnolia
May-June—Arkansas-Oklahoma Rodeo, Fort Smith
June—Pink Tomato Festival, Warren
June—Turtle Derby, Gould
June—Fulton County Old Timers Day and Singing Convention, Salem
July—Chicken Fry, Mount Nebo
August—Tontitown Grape Festival, Springdale
August—Fish Fry, Grady
September—Frontier Frolics, Bull Shoals
September—Arkansas-Oklahoma Livestock Exhibition and District Free
          Fair, Fort Smith
September—Saunders Museum Muzzle Shoot, Berryville
September—Terrapin Derby, Lepanto
September—Four State Fair and Rodeo, Texarkana
September—Oil Belt Golf Tournament, El Dorado
October—National Cotton Picking Contest, Blytheville
October—National Medieval Crossbow Tournament, Huntsville
October—Ozark Folk Festival, Eureka Springs
October—Tanico Festival of Art, Hot Springs
October—National Wild Turkey Calling Contest and Turkey Trot,
          Yellville
October—Arkansas Livestock Exposition, Little Rock
October—Ozark Arts and Crafts Fair, War Eagle
November—Festival of Art, Pine Bluff
November—World Championship Duck Calling Contest and Agricultural
          Festival, Stuttgart
November—National Hunting Dog Field Trials, Booneville
December—Pool of Siloam Christmas Pageant, Siloam Springs
December—Columbia County Christmas Pageant, Magnolia
December—Christmas Parade and Christmas Eve Pageant, Hot Springs

90

Thinkers, Doers, Fighters

Burns, Bob
Caraway, Hattie W.
Catlin, George
Cleburne, Patrick R.
Fletcher, John Gould
French, Alice (Octave Thanet)
Fulbright, James William
Garland, Augustus
Guess, George (Sequoya)
Harvey, William Hope
Hindman, Thomas C.
Hunt, H.L.

MacArthur, Douglas
McCormic, Mary
Mills, Wilbur D.
Parker, Isaac
Pike, Albert
Robinson, Joseph T.
Sarasen (Chief)
Stanley, Henry Morton
Still, William Grant
Takatoka (Chief)
Washburn, Edward Payson
Yell, Archibald

Governors of the State of Arkansas

James Conway, 1836-1840
Archibald Yell, 1840-1844
Thomas Drew, 1844-1849
John S. Roane, 1849-1852
Elias N. Conway, 1852-1860
Henry M. Rector, 1860-1862
Harris Flanagin, 1862-1864
Isaac Murphy, 1864-1868
Powell Clayton, 1868-1871
Ozra A. Hadley, 1871-1873
Elisha Baxter, 1873-1874
Augustus H. Garland, 1874-1877
William R. Miller, 1877-1881
Thomas J. Churchill, 1881-1883
James H. Berry, 1883-1885
Simon P. Hughes, 1885-1889
James P. Eagle, 1889-1893
William M. Fishback, 1893-1895
James P. Clark, 1895-1897
Daniel W. Jones, 1897-1901

Jeff Davis, 1901-1907
John S. Little, 1907-1909
George W. Donaghey, 1909-1913
Joseph T. Robinson, 1913
George W. Hays, 1913-1917
Charles H. Brough, 1917-1921
Thomas C. McRae, 1921-1925
Thomas J. Terral, 1925-1927
John E. Martineau, 1927-1928
Harvey Parnell, 1928-1933
J.M. Futrell, 1933-1937
Carl E. Bailey, 1937-1941
Homer M. Adkins, 1941-1945
Benjamin Laney, 1945-1949
Sidney McMath, 1949-1953
Francis Cherry, 1953-1955
Orval E. Faubus, 1955-1967
Winthrop Rockefeller, 1967-1971
Dale L. Bumpers, 1971-1975
David Pryor, 1975-

Index

92

94

95

PICTURE CREDITS

ABOUT THE AUTHOR

With the publication of his first book for school use when he was twenty, **Allan Carpenter** began a career as an author that has spanned more than 135 books. After teaching in the public schools of Des Moines, Mr. Carpenter began his career as an educational publisher at the age of twenty-one when he founded the magazine *Teachers Digest*. In the field of educational periodicals, he was responsible for many innovations. During his many years in publishing, he has perfected a highly organized approach to handling large volumes of factual material: after extensive traveling and having collected all possible materials, he systematically reviews and organizes everything. From his apartment high in Chicago's John Hancock Building, Allan recalls, "My collection and assimilation of materials on the states and countries began before the publication of my first book." Allan is the founder of Carpenter Publishing House and of Infordata International, Inc., publishers of *Issues in Education* and *Index to U. S. Government Periodicals*. When he is not writing or traveling, his principal avocation is music. He has been the principal bassist of many symphonies, and he managed the country's leading non-professional symphony for twenty-five years.